Minóy

Minóy

Joseph Nechvatal, editor

dead letter office

BABEL Working Group

punctum books ∗ brooklyn, ny

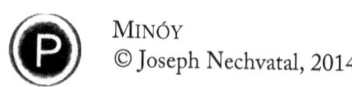

MINÓY
© Joseph Nechvatal, 2014

http://creativecommons.org/licenses/by-nc-nd/3.0/

This work is Open Access, which means that you are free to copy, distribute, display, and perform the work as long as you clearly attribute the work to the authors, that you do not use this work for commercial gain in any form whatsoever, and that you in no way alter, transform, or build upon the work outside of its normal use in academic scholarship without express permission of the author and the publisher of this volume. For any reuse or distribution, you must make clear to others the license terms of this work.

First published in 2014 by
dead letter office, BABEL Working Group
an imprint of punctum books
Brooklyn, New York
http://punctumbooks.com

Companion CD and cassette tape available at
http://www.punctumrecords.com/minoy/

The BABEL Working Group is a collective and desiring-assemblage of scholar-gypsies with no leaders or followers, no top and no bottom, and only a middle. BABEL roams and stalks the ruins of the post-historical university as a multiplicity, a pack, looking for other roaming packs with which to cohabit and build temporary shelters for intellectual vagabonds. We also take in strays.

ISBN-13: 978-0692234273
ISBN-10: 0692234276

Cover Image: *Minóy as Haint as King Lear* (photo by Maya Eidolon/Amber Sabri).

TABLE OF CONTENTS

// 1

Mongram
The Saturated Superimposed Agency of Minóy

Joseph Nechvatal

// 19

Mémoire
Whatever Happened to the Man Named Minóy?

Amber Sabri

Portfolio
Minóy as Haint as King Lear

Maya Eidolon

// 63

After Words
The Obscurity of Minóy

Joseph Nechvatal

// 71

After After Words
The Aesthetics of an Obscure Monster Sacré

Joseph Nechvatal

// 85

After After After Words
Hyper Noise Aesthetics

Joseph Nechvatal

Monogram

THE SATURATED SUPERIMPOSED AGENCY OF MINÓY

Joseph Nechvatal

What chaos and rhythm have in common is the in-between—
between two milieus, rhythm-chaos or the chaosmos: Between
night and day, between that which is constructed and that
which grows naturally, between mutations from the inorganic
to the organic, from plant to animal, from animal to human-
kind, yet without this series constituting a progression. In this
in-between, chaos becomes rhythm, not inexorably, but it has
a chance to. Chaos is not the opposite of rhythm, but the
milieu of all milieus.
   Gilles Deleuze and Félix Guattari, *A Thousand Plateaus*

AN INTRODUCTION

Minóy was the pseudonym of the electronic art musician
and sound artist Stanley Keith Bowsza (October 30, 1951-

March 19, 2010). Until now, it was thought that he stopped recording in 1992.

Minóy created some of the most remarkably engrossing, beautiful and imaginative art music albums released on cassette in the 1980s, often with handmade covers mailed out from his home in Torrance, California. Though perhaps understandably unknown to you, the reader (he was celebrated only once, in 1991, when his image appeared on the cover of the July 1991 issue of Electronic Cottage magazine), Minóy was a major figure in the DIY-controlled noise music and homemade independent cassette culture scene of the 1980s.

It is significant that Bowsza chose his pseudonym Minóy based upon how someone he met mispronounced the name of one of his favorite artists, the deceased Catalan Surrealist Joan Miró. One can detect with this choice early on his embrace of psychic chance operations coupled to the phantasmagorical; a method-theme that is profoundly explored during his creative career.

Minóy was agoraphobic, but a prolific sound artist intensely active in the music underground between the years 1986 and 1992. During that period he created many mesmerizing audio agglomerations in collaboration with other sound artists and mail artists. To be sure, Minóy was an avid mail collaborator, working with noted experimental American composers such as PBK (Phillip B. Klingler) (as Minóy and PBK but also as Disco Splendor), If, Bwana (as Bwannoy), Agog (as No Mail On Sundays), Zan Hoffman (as Minóy/Zannóy), Dave Prescott (as PM), Not 1/2 (as El Angel Exterminador), and many others.

But he is best known for his thick palimpsest-like multi-tracked soundscape solo compositions: productions that follow the incorporation of multilayered electric sound into music compositional practice similar, at times, to the masterful musique concrète of the Groupe de Recherches Musicales.

In general, his noise music is a form of labyrinthian droning superimposed collage electronics that produced an immersive otherworldly effect. It is a form of highly textured, manipulated, and layered sound and noise that often creates a sonic painting-like effect with a spatial feel. Frequently, nonperiodic tone clusters sweep across the treble range, moving the contours of the sound, like shifting waves of shimmering colors that glide in an ocean of found sound. Many of his tape releases had only one or two compositions on them, thus allowing him the time to develop a drone theme and hypnotically immerse the listener in what were vastly complex works of art.

His challenging, irritating at times, roaring-ambient recordings were often created by delay echoing and multi-tracking sounds (like field recordings and short wave transmissions), forming these sounds into deep and blurry ambiguous compositions full of feeling. Sometimes he used a constant murmuring voice along with found sounds or static or shrieks or staccato guitar bursts or the twitter of a toy mouth organ. His commanding but graceful compositions were more often than not delicate yet powerfully embellished soundscapes of great artistic sophistication. The work's transformative affect is typically achieved through an effective cumulative buildup of tense, almost nervous, sounds that cycle through the realm of overload, an overload that compresses and mutates the original sound sources and transforms them into an expanding and indeterminate sonic field. It is a technique of creative destruction highly suggestive of forms of social resistance applicable to global techno-culture, as it suggests an ultimate triumph of individual originality over national-corporate hegemony.

A GHOSTLY REFLECTION

Minóy's lingering sonic material is a project of personal transformation (for him and us) that also covers much of the sonorous scope of the second half of the 20th Century, expanding the boundaries of the musical exploration of complex overtone structures. Minóy was (and is still) a precise example of expansive post-John Cagian abstract sound-music let loose upon the expanding electronic environment in which we now abide. Of course, Minóy's sample-based sound-music is noise music, indeed. It's often a bit antagonistic, irritating and sometimes unpleasant, but it's also exceedingly considered and put together beautifully with the utmost proficiency and comprehension. Yet a listener must fabricate a complicated forensic fairy-tale out of its counter-mannerist mélange as it keeps slipping in and out of idiosyncratic narration.

Minóy's compositions are both harsh and contemplative. The contemplative register of his layered sound-music, achieved through superimposition as opposed to juxtaposition (for example in 'Doctor In A Dark Room'), is noticeably different from other sample-based audio artists, such as the early sonic collage works of John Cage ('Williams Mix,' 1952, 'Fontana Mix,' 1958-59 and 'Rozart Mix,' 1965), James Tenney ('Collage #1–Blue Suede,' 1961), Steve Reich ('Come Out,' 1966), Terry Riley ('You're No Good,' 1967), Negativland, John Oswald ('Plunderphonics'), or Christian Marclay. I find Minóy's superimposed sound aesthetic closer to that of the audio décollage work of Wolf Vostell. Indeed, I feel that his droning fluttering work sounds closer to that of Vostell and to some early work of Pierre Schaeffer ('Cinq Etudes De Bruits: Etude Violette,' 1948), John Cage ('Radio Music,' 1956), Pierre Henry ('Après La Mort 2: Mouvement En 6 Parties,' 1967), and La Monte Young ('Two Sounds,' 1960, 'Poem For Tables Chairs Etc., Parts 1 & 2,' 1960, and '23 VIII 64 2:50:45 – 3:11 am, The Volga Delta From Studies In The Bowed Disc,' 1969). Indeed, though exactly the opposite of La Monte in one way (Minóy's released public output was prodigious—perhaps only surpassed by that of Merzbow— and La Monte's is tiny), like La

Monte, duration (time in terms of the distribution of flows) plays a large part in his compositions of assembly. And like La Monte, their lengthy layered complexity is a neurological stimulant for the imagination. The extended length allows deep subjective perceptions of the present moment to come to consciousness. As such, they offer a sonically ontological vision of the world as superimposition, one that shows us in place inside of a saturated world. Thus a mental picture in which both the human and the nonhuman are recognized as open-ended becoming: a mental place where we take on emergent forms in an intrinsically temporal play of agency.

In that sense (for me), Minóy's noise music can be heard as a superimposed block of philosophical propositions that immerse us into rather different conceptions of being in the world. Here we are expected to work devotedly to appreciate its absurd conundrums, and to supply mental transitions between the diverse assortments of irrational elements that supply the sound-music its hooks.

As a matter of fact, Minóy conjures up a different ontological interplay of the human and the nonhuman, as his productions speak powerfully of a dense, embodied, material engagement with the world at large. The sound of Minóy has us listen to (and look for) pure visceral abandonment coupled with emergent aesthetic effects in the world (superimposed swirls and vortices of chance juxtapositions, for example), which allows us to be carried away to a place where we are at once both the psychic co-author and the detached explorer of his composition, both an active and passive player at work in constructing its connotation. This is one key point I really want to emphasize, how Minóy unarguably shows us how originality based in co-directional creativity can still genuinely emerge in our digital age of endlessly recycled culture by remaining in the thick of things. With Minóy we go to the superimpositional place of the intersection of the actual and the virtual, and the human and the nonhuman, in an open-ended, forward-looking, search process. Subsequently I would say, Minóy's sonic material thematizes for us a thick ontology of layered becoming, as it entails an assembly between the human (us now) and the nonhuman (the work he left behind), as well as an intrinsically sequential and superimpositional becoming-at-large.

The point to grasp is: to appreciate Minóy's droning style of assembly depends on us living in the thick of things. And his labyrinthian electronic sounds thematizes that assembly for us.

On the other hand, the haunting 2007-2009 portrait images from the 'Minóy as Haint as King Lear' series that photographer Maya Eidolon created before his death in collaboration with Minóy (then known as Haint) and Stuart Hass (Minóy's partner)—included as an image portfolio in this volume—visually thematizes for us the eerie madness of resisting that ontological condition of existence. At this point, I have to say something about 'Minóy as Haint as King Lear' that has in one way or another helped me live in the presence of becoming. 'Minóy as Haint as King Lear' unites life and death visually in a counter-hegemonic formation full of self-conscious unifying practices. Thus Eidolon's photographs point me in the direction of a natural ontological attitude, exposing dualist detachment from the world for what it is: just one tactic of being in the fluxing world that we have at our disposal, and that is always slipping away from us.

It is salient that Bowsza took on a third pseudonym for this phantasmal project of self-invention: Haint (he dropped the name Minóy and stopped releasing recordings in 1992) as 'haint' is a deep-south American colloquialism for a ghost, apparition, or lost soul. A general point I want to make here about 'Minóy as Haint as King Lear' is that we should not be dazzled by the work's phantasmagorical field. Instead of seeing this performance for the camera as a descent into the thick eerie nonhuman (or as a move, a tactic, a ploy, a play), we should perhaps see the performance as a very specific way of living mad in the intensified flow of superimposed becoming. After all, we can well imagine his rage against his approaching death here. We can almost hear in these images his Lear-like scream into an unbounded white noise.

Thus for me, Bowsza in 'Minóy as Haint as King Lear' delivers an airy irrational punch of nonsensical negation to spectral life by tying together methods of insouciant informality with a visceral irony: at turns hip and flamboyant or abrasively outrageous. And, alas, that recitation keeps turning back into one about stinking death—that strange, incurable and deeply irrational affliction. So yes, 'Minóy as Haint as King Lear' is about self-transcendence by means of madness. Indeed I read it as a meditation on humiliating death in all its undifferentiated fabulousness, by which I mean its essentially nasty comedy. 'Minóy as Haint as King Lear' is then crazy counter-mannerist art about comical, difficult death. So my argument is that even if we live and die in the thick of virtual *and* actual de-centred processes of becoming human and nonhuman, this is normally veiled from us by a particular tactic of dualist detachment and Bowsza tears back that veil.

To move in this direction with 'Minóy as Haint as King Lear' also immediately reminds us that in an ontology of becoming, art shades indirectly (and perhaps, also, unconsciously) into spirituality as immanent in nature, which itself is to be wondered at. Utter energy or vitalist matter: either way, with 'Minóy as Haint as King Lear' we are in an enormous artistic and spiritual field that immediately evokes the ontology of becoming of Gilles Deleuze. 'Minóy as Haint as King Lear' is self-consciously in the flow of becoming a phantasmal self-experiment, imaginatively exploring the open-ended spaces of the world's possibility. So this is where I would look for inspiration to renew our ontological faculties to remake the phantom world again, materially as well as representationally.

A Remembrance (from afar)

As for most others, Minóy first came into my realm of awareness in the mail. I never met the man. Out of the blue I received in my Lower East Side mailbox a tape from him that I loved immediately: 'In Search Of Tarkovsky.' I quickly began trading *Tellus Audio Cassette Magazine*[1] tapes with him for his work; my favorites being 'Doctor In A Dark Room' (1985), 'Nightslaves' (1986) and 'Firebird' (1987). These tapes resonated considerably with the overloaded nature of the palimpsest-like gray graphite drawings I was working on then (which were reflective of the time's concerns around multiple forms of proliferation). But my reception of his music also had to do with my vague impressions of California. No, there was no sun in them, but I could vaguely detect the vastness of the Pacific Ocean, long LSD trips, morning bong hits, and lurking danger; something like listening to the Beach Boys' 'Pet Sounds' while on bad acid. So I was deeply impressed by his talent on those tapes even without meeting him, and I was determined to publish something by him on *Tellus* as soon as I could.

His work reminded me of when I first saw the obscure No Wave performer Boris Policeband play his screechy sounds in 1978 at a concert to benefit Colab's *X Magazine*. It was entrancing for me how Policeband appropriated police scanner radio transmissions, entwining them with his dissonant violin and hilarious voice. After Rhys Chatham, his brand of post-minimalism may have had the greatest influence on my striving for my own form of post-minimal chaos magic, an art of magical gazing.

That year I had been reading Aleister Crowley's book *Magick in Theory and Practice*. What I conjectured from Crowley while listening and watching Boris Policeband, was

---

[1] See "Tellus Audio Cassette Magazine," *Wikipedia*, http://en.wikipedia.org/wiki/Tellus_Audio_Cassette_Magazine.

that a noisy aesthetic visualization process could be used to create feedback optic stimulus to the neocortex in a kind of cop-free project of foreseeing (an attempt to scan into an un-policed future), based roughly on the basis of magical gazing. That gazing idea led me to form *Tellus Audio Cassette Magazine* and hence become acquainted with the music of Minóy.

Tellus Audio Cassette Magazine was created in 1983 by me, curator Claudia Gould, and Carol Parkinson, a composer and staff member of Harvestworks/Studio PASS. We met for drinks to discuss my idea of a magazine on cassette that would feature interesting and challenging sound works. With the advent of the Walkman and the Boom Box, we perceived a need for an alternative to overdetermined radio programming and the commercially available recordings on the market at that time. We then began to collect, produce, document and define the art of audio by publishing works from local, national and international artists. Sometimes we worked with contributing editors, experts in their fields, who proposed themes and collected the best works from that genre. Unknown artists were teamed with well-known artists, historical works were juxtaposed with contemporary ones, and high art with popular art, all in an effort to enhance the crossover communication between the different mediums of art: visual, music, performance, and spoken word.

I was very pleased to have published Minóy's dark ambient composition 'Tango' in 1988 as the lead piece on Side B of *Tellus* #20, an issue that I curated, entitled 'Media Myth.' The premise behind 'Media Myth' arrived to me out of the compositional principles of my palimpsest graphite drawings (deeply layered and saturated with vague imagery) in contact with the shivering layered fuzz music of Minóy. I would often do my artwork with Minóy playing on the Walkman headset or blasting out from my black Boom Box.

Slowly the goal of the 'Media Myth' issue became the

exploration of the introspective world of the ear under the influence of the era's high-frequency electronic environment —that is, electronic circulation. Since it was rather difficult making sense of the mid-1980s swirling media society, the general proposition behind Media Myth was to look for a paradoxical summation of this uncertainty by looking for artists who took advantage of the time's superficial saturation—a saturation so dense that it failed to communicate anything particular at all upon which we could concur (except perhaps its overall incomprehensible sense of ripe delirium) as the Reaganomic reproduction system pulsed with higher and higher, and faster and faster, flows of senseless info-data to the point of ear hysteria.

Perhaps the result of this ripe information abundance was that, the greater the amount of Reaganomic information that flowed, the greater the incredulity which it produced—at least, for thinking, questioning artists. So, the tremendous load of data produced and reproduced all around us then ultimately seemed to make less, not more, conventional sense. Indeed, this freeing feeling became the premise of the 'Media Myth' issue.

This supposition, it now seems to me, played also into the history of abstract art which teaches us that art may refuse to recognize all thought as existing in the form of representation, and that by scanning the spread of representation, art may formulate a critique of the laws that provide representation with its organizational basis. As a result, in my view, it was electronic-based sound art's onus to see what unconventional, paradoxical, summational sense (in terms of the subjective world of the imagination) art might make of the mid-1980s based on an appropriately decadent reading of the time's paradoxically material-based (yet electronically activated) media environment.

Such a basically abstract, artistic, paradoxical/summational fancy began with the presumption that an information-loaded nuclear weapon had already exploded, showering me with bits of radioactive-like informational sound bytes, thus drastically changing the way in which I perceived and acted, even in my subconscious dream world. Perhaps you can now see why Minóy's 'In Search Of Tarkovsky' touched me so deeply, as Andrei Tarkovsky's film *Stalker* (1979) is a reasonable zone of connection to these ideas and feelings, as seven years after the making of the film, the Chernobyl disaster occurred (on April 26, 1986) and that led to the depopulation of a surrounding area that was officially called the zone of alienation, rather like in the *Stalker* film.

Minóy's weirdly romantic sound, by virtue of its distinctive electronic constitution of fluidity, floated for me in an extensive stratosphere of circulation while also simultaneously being tied to the materiality of the physical ribbon in the cassette tape. Hence, the particular constitution of Minóy superimposing and overflowing compositions could best be seen, perhaps even more so today, as an osmotic membrane: a blotter of the instantaneous ubiquity/proliferation of the mid 1980s. Consequently, Minóy reflected (and worked with) the social power that was shaped by the de-centered electronic overload of the 1980s. This is its historical merit.

So, the question for the 'Media Myth' issue of *Tellus* was: how could artists like Minóy and I symbolically turn these de-centered power codes into artistic abstractions of social merit? Perhaps it was possible because he knew, and demonstrated with 'Tango,' that these symbolic media codes, which after all, helter-skelter, make us up as representational characters, are positively phantasmagorical.

This is, of course, even more true today.

Based on the premises of his atypical 'Tango,' perhaps a socially relevant digitally-based creativity can still be found dancing in today's electronic world. After all, electrons partake (and make up) the all-encompassing phantasmagorical/ technological sign-field within which we live and which defines us (at least in part). Conventional non-artistic representation is often thought constructed of rather solid, unyielding social signs. Fine art, like Minóy's 'Tango,' typically is thought to be made up of dancing, anti-social, unconventional, irresponsible signs. For me, 'Tango,' though constructed from social signs (albeit abused), represented the fine art mode of weird dark realism that corresponds to the real arbitrary nature of all signs, subverting socially controlled systems of meaning. In Minóy's electronic noise I heard the opportunity for the creation of applicable anti-social phantasmagorical signs. That and abstract ecstatic anti-signs, that continue to mentally move and multiply within. Such a Tango-based, fancied aesthetic non-knowledge is certainly the most erudite, the most aware, the most conscious area of our current identity, as it is also the phantasmal depths from which all digital representation emerges in its precarious, but glittering, existence.

Indeed, it was this quivering phantasmal cohesion found in his un-danceable 'Tango' (and in his weirdly sublime/perverse output in general) that maintained for me a way beyond reductive conceptual minimalism into an excessive post-conceptualism. 'Tango' is an early example of a post-media art, which is in theory, opposed to the tabular mental space laid out by classical thought. It is an art where reproduction technologies blur into transformations continually laced with contradictory messages (and that necessarily counters the logic of crisp information), warped and rowdy shifts in scale that evokes the infinite, and unexpected woven interconnections between the micro and the macro.

If the ultra-dissemination of the physiological signs in 'Tango' may create such phantasmagorical hyper-logics of use to the formation of art, his potential may prove useful in questioning received notions of representation when viewed against assumptions of utility versus pleasure. Indeed, perhaps his unconscious intention with 'Tango' was to achieve an ultimate phantasmal integration by dissolving audio form into its original electronic foundation of nerve energy.

Such a dynamic sense of aesthetic electronica as nervous contemplative vision might suggest the continued potential of social re-configuration, as it subsumes our previous world of simulation/representation into a phantasmagorical nexus of overlapping, linked hybrid observations of the outer world with precise extractions of human mentality. Encounters, then, with his audio work, one may assume, might create an opportunity for symbolic societal transgression, and for a vertiginous ecstasy of thought.

Surely such an electronica/phantasmal impetus as found in his artistic production can help release pent-up ecstatic energies today, in that the more overwhelming and restrictive the social mechanism becomes in our age of digital surveillance, the more noisy the counter-effects needed. Hence he pushes us to exceed the assumed determinism of the technological-based phenomenon inherent (supposedly) in our post-industrial information society. Therefore, his electronic music may serve as an ecstatic impulse/phenomena which proliferates in proportion to the technicization of society. As such, a nervous electronica-ecstasy may emerge as a result of our technological society's obsession with the phantasmal character of digital speed and proliferation.

Predictions for his legacy, then: as human psychic energies are stifled and/or bypassed by certain controlling aspects of mass digital data-mining, such nervously frenzied art like his will increasingly break out in forms of noisy resonances (and noisy visuals) that will promote an indispensable alienation from the socially constructed. His is a necessary outburst of nervy ecstatic art superimposed onto data-mined experience. Thus his type of noisy euphoric counterattack, such as in 'Corridors' (1985), provides phantasmal defiance through transport aimed against the controlling world's scrutiny-destructiveness. Consequently, his aesthetic philosophy will provide a fundamental antithesis to the authoritarian, perfunctory, simulated rigidities of the controlling technical world.

I would ultimately argue that the nervous phantasmal play found in his noisescapes has urgent political/social ramifications in our media saturated digital society today. His well-founded phantasmal model for an art of noise indicates the continued capacity for the electronic media's worth, as it provides the explication and the means of the nervous phantasmal links that abet both communications and the superimposition of becoming onto being. Hence, his excessive audio abstractions, such as those found in his pieces 'Mass' or 'Shame On Love' (both 1986), or with Zan Hoffman as Minóy/Zannoy, 'Why Jake Hobo Ate Whey' (1987), can be seen and heard, in a sense, as the representation of all representation when we attempt to think through an artistic unlimited field of representation as non-utilitarian phantasmal ideology. This would be an attempt at scrutinizing representation in accordance with the sound's phantasmal non-discursive process as noise music, such as in his 'Distant Thoughts' or 'The Last Fortune Cookie' (both 1986), where he has demonstrated for us art as an abstract Object-Oriented metaphysics—a nerve-based metaphysics where his phantasmal noises helps us step outside of ourselves and to posit ourselves outside of the mechanics of homogeneous dogmatisms.

And so Minóy: the spectral audio project I have outlined for you based in part on your posthumous work 'Pawbone Kisser Daylight Sins I' (1993), will, I hope, contribute to the inventing of a new nervous noise art in which what matters is no longer sound identities, or logos, but rather dense, phantasmagorical forces developed on the basis of inclusion. A project where from now on things will be heard and seen only from the depths of this reverberating inclusive density (withdrawn into itself, perhaps, and adumbrated and darkened by its obscurity), but bound tightly together and inescapably grouped by the vigor that is hidden in a depth that is fermenting a phantasmagorical discourse that is both nervously capricious and, paradoxically, socially responsible.

ADDENDUM: CRITICAL DESCRIPTION & RECEPTION OF VARIOUS RELEASES

'White With a Crust Of Chill'
Thick layers of sounds added together make a detailed and overwhelming mix. Most of the tapes from Minóy have a distinct sound, sort of like high-pitched machine noises with bits of different musics wafting in and out of focus. Excellent, Must hear. (Robin James, *Sound Choice* #5, 1986)

'Obscure Medicines'
Have you ever screwed up something so bad or got caught doing something so embarrassing that the memory of it, even years later, is physically painful? Well, Minóy has just composed a sound collage for you if you have. The opening track, 'Naked Came The Memory,' begins with mechanical chattering, industrial pounding, a stringed instrument suffering rape and torture, and a haunting drone that sounds like a far off air raid siren stuck on a middle tone. All this builds up, ebbs away and then comes back full in your face like the naked truths we must face from time to time. On the title track it sounds like every stringed instrument in Torrance, California tuning up in Minóy's living room until the sounds swirl and rotate about each other like some discordant tornado. Five more equally disturbing or masochistically pleasing tunes follow, perfect background music when your Uncle Bob overstays his welcome, drinks the last shot of Old Thompson and still won't go home. (Mick Mather, *Sound Choice* #9, 1987)

'Plain Wrap Purgatory'
An acknowledged master of sound collage offers two side-long pieces, the title cut and 'Flying Overhead.' For the un-

initiated, this is the guy who lives under your bed and creates soundtracks for your worst nightmares. Purgatory greets the listener with disembodied voices, moans, groans, demonic howling, clanging, industrial drones, and a stringed instrument tinkling like windchimes from hell, er, purgatory. These sounds are layered, bent, treated and kicked in and out of the mix, a Minóy trademark. On side two it appears our sins have been purged. We're treated to an airy, uplifting blend of sound, giving the impression that you might be flying and making that last connection out of purgatory. Then, en route to some higher place the tone begins to turn brooding and ominous once more, like ice forming on the wings . . . Mary, Mother of GOD, full of grace . . . . (Mick Mather, *Sound Choice* #9, 1987)

'Pretty Young Negro Man'

More kooky, psychotic, and truly hellish sounds from this prolific sound composer. Followed immediately by loud, high-pitched machine interruptions. Groans, drones and warps loop in and out of sequence. Found sounds from many sources are woven into the irregular rhythm of the piece. A severely distorted string instrument is being beaten to death and gives out horrific, inhuman cries. There's also some of the strangest vocal manipulations I've ever heard. On side two Minóy plays with the radio dial, turning it slowly to catch extended bits of random speech and Mexican music, and turning it quickly to get clicks and honks. It's as if several radios are shot through a tremendous p.a. system. A peaceful, yet oddly disturbing synth is laid on top. The overall mood is alarming, playful and determined. (Christopher Carstens, *Sound Choice* #9, 1987)

'Firebird' & 'The Flavor Of Acid On Ice'

Minóy is one of the stalwart figures of the cassette network. At last count there were 63 tapes available and an untold number of collaborations and compilation appearances. These are two relatively recent releases. On both Minóy builds surging/droning looping icicle shaped sound pictures out of minimal electronics. I prefer the earlier Firebird for it's more varied moods. Morning is especially evocative. That's when I enjoy his music the most, in the morning, as sun cuts in low across the room. Sound mingles with dust particles floating in a beam. 'The Flavor Of Acid On Ice' gets a bit more violent in its imagery. Both are capable of producing these visual pictures through sound. (Glen Thrasher, *Lowlife* 13, 1988)

'Doctor In A Dark Room' & 'Babel'
Two 30-minute pieces of unique textural richness, borrowing something from industrial, Ligeti, Xenakis, and Tangerine Dream. 'Doctor In A Dark Room' creates a mesmerizing effect by constantly hovering between tone and noise, disembodied orchestras and choirs singing multi-timbral drones, crashing waves of sound . . . best at high volume, but not late at night. 'Babel' is multi-tracked radios (FM, AM, Shortwave, CB, etc.), voices wreaking havoc with meaning and intelligibility in a dense riot of glossolalia. I'd call Minóy a maximalist as he is unafraid of thick and heavy textures which could run the risk of collapsing upon themselves. (Tom Furgas, *Option Magazine*, Jan/Feb 1985)

'Future Perfect'
This consistently engaging tape plays tricks on your perceptions by displaying large sheets of texture that overlap one another so that it becomes impossible to discern whether they are organic or synthetic. Under this he further confounds us with barely perceptible voices that haunt from afar. Filled with a strange beauty, it evokes images of imaginary landscapes. (Kim Cascone, *Option Magazine*, Jan/ Feb 1985)

'Landscape With Serpent'
More great sonic mayhem from the master of the musically

macabre. On side A, 'Stalker' is that presence following you down that ciurcuitous tunnel to hell. Programmatic isn't a dirty word, but for the most part, this surpasses that and is just plain eerie. The title side evokes visions of a primordial wasteland with a menagerie of strange, lumbering life-forms cavorting way off in the (safe) distance. In the closing section, the serpent's lonely wails penetrate the heavy mist and fog. (Jack Jordan, *Option Magazine*, Sept/Oct 1987)

Mémoire

WHATEVER HAPPENED TO THE MAN NAMED MINÓY?

A Mémoire of My Dearest Friend, Stanley Keith Bowsza, the Man Who Was Minóy

Amber Sabri

BEYOND LOVE STORIES

Love is a Madman working his wild schemes, tearing off his clothes, drinking poison, and now quietly choosing annihilation. A tiny spider tries to wrap an enormous wasp. Think of the spiderweb woven across the cave. There are love stories and there is obliteration into love. Love flows down. The ground submits to the sky and suffers what comes. Open completely. Let your spirit ear listen to the green dome's passionate murmur. Let the cords of your robe be untied. Shiver in this new love beyond all above and below.

The sun rises but which way does the night go?

I have no more words. Let the soul speak with the silent articulation of a face.

> Locked out of life, waiting, weeping.
> Coleman Barks, *A Year with Rumi: Daily Readings*

The man who was the noiseMusic and cassette artist named Minóy disappeared completely from public view in 1992. In this memoir I would like to acquaint you, dear reader, with a brief history of the man who was Minóy so that perhaps the mystery of his sudden exodus can be understood.

I first virtually met Stanley Keith Bowsza through Flickr, the well-known image sharing website. I joined the site in January of 2005 and began uploading my photos and artwork under the name of Maya Eidolon. About a month later, someone named "My Life as A Haint" effusively complimented my digital art. When I looked at his Flickr site of artwork, I was in absolute awe. Our friendship grew from this moment. We began to comment on each other's work, share ideas and communicate through private Flickr mail. We were both eccentric and we were similar in so many ways.

Haint made light photoPaintings, and this grabbed me as the first photos I had made as a teenager were black and white light paintings of moving traffic at night. We both loved motion and blur and the night. Haint called us the Neon Night Twins.

Through the summer and early fall of 2005, we communicated intensely via Flickr mail. We trusted each other and he needed someone to talk to, someone to confide in. He was entertaining and funny and a wonderful storyteller.

We shared a certain approach to our creative work. Keith Bowsza, both as Minóy the musician and as Haint the artist, worked intuitively with a minimum of pre-planning. The work evolved and was refined over time. It is my belief that what defines an artist is the richness and unique formation of the artist's intuition (a 'sixth' sense), an amalgam of conscious, unconscious and subconscious thoughts and feelings and bits and snippets of sound and image. The ongoing jumbleMemory of one's life is the well from where intuition and creative endeavor flow.

To me, that intuition can best be visualized as a cosmos, a structure so large that one can not see its outside edges because the moment one begins to try to conceive of the enormity of it, the moment one tries to imagine what it might look like if it were possible to be outside it at a huge distance, one becomes engulfed within and swept along the glistening arrays of molecular structures, ever-shifting with light and color illuminating the impenetrable surrounding darkness.

Keith sought to channel his intuition and be carried along by his creation whilst he created it. That process provided gratification for him and he wanted his audience to share the delicious and profound phantasmagoric depth of feeling and emotion he experienced as he created the work.

The power of Keith's creative output came from his prodigious resources. He was often manic: he barely slept and he spent most of his functional waking hours either producing art or absorbing art, music, or film. He had a phenomenal memory for sound and imagery, and when he created sound he approached it like he approached everything else, intuitively with gargantuan passion and leviathan intensity. The sounds he wanted to produce were the soundNoise music of his inner experience, not to be gently orchestrated but screaming to be let out: colossal sweeps of multilayered feeling and turbulent emotions. He created what he was feeling and the core of what he was feeling was mammoth psychic and physical pain. Being the terrific showman that he was, he knew how to maximize the effects and with his flare for drama, he played it to the hilt.

We were mutually simpatico from the moment we met and I was instantly smitten with this marvelous man and his work. He was brilliant and had a vast Brobdingnagian knowledge of art as well as music, film and theater. He was a sensitive and beautiful soul: intense and passionate. We became the dearest of friends. He delighted in being my entertainment director, sending me music and recommending films.

Keith shared with me that he was an invalid confined to a wheelchair with little respite from his decades long struggles with neuropathic pain, frequent episodes of intractable panic, and the mania and paranoia that had permeated his daily life. Always a large man, he had become morbidly obese. By this time in his life he was rarely able to muster the stamina to leave the house. He lived on his bed, surrounded by CDs, DVDs and art books. His computer was his link to the outside world.

I believe that it was a catastrophic event early in his life that greatly influenced Keith's personality and outlook towards the world. In his late teenage years, Keith told his parents he was gay. They responded with what was an all-too-common reaction in those days: they thought he needed to be "cured." In a horrifyingly misguided attempt to "fix" his homosexuality, they subjected him to sessions of electroconvulsive therapy (ECT). He complied willingly at first, but after he accidentally died and had to be resuscitated on the ECT table during one of these electroshock procedures, he refused to continue. This dreadful episode clearly had profound effects on his mind and body. All of his life he had terrifying nightmares, reliving an out-of-body experience of death, and seeing the "white light."

Although he told me that he had forgiven his parents for this abysmal act of parental treachery masked as compassion and love, issues of fear and betrayal plagued him throughout his life. He remained keenly sensitive to betrayal, real and/or imagined. Pain, panic, paranoia, bipolar mania, schizophrenia . . . he lived it all. Massive amounts of medications had been prescribed for him for more than forty years in an effort to mitigate his neuropathic pain and psychic suffering, beginning with antidepressives in his adolescence, and he had to cope with side effects as well.

As 2005 progressed, my friendship with Keith deepened profoundly. We spoke every day. Sometime in early October I awoke and went to my computer eager to view my usual morning treat of looking at the new images Haint had uploaded. To my great horror, his whole account was gone. My heart sank and I started to panic. My visceral gut reaction was fear that I had lost touch with this incredible man. I lived in San Francisco and he lived in Los Angeles. All of our communication had been via Flickr and now I had no way to reach him. I was bereft. My heart was broken. Much to my relief, after a few hours Keith phoned me and assured me he didn't want to lose touch either.

That morning when I discovered Keith had deleted his entire art and photo website on Flickr, I thought perhaps he had done so in a fit of despairing rage and desolate fury, but I was wrong. He told me he had been contemplating it for several weeks, resisting the urge. His feeling was that if he performed this act of self-assassination it would in some way free him . . . and yes, he was right . . . it seemed to work for him. He felt better.

During the next few years Haint's ritual of self-annihilation was to be repeated several more times, echoing his disappearance of Minóy in 1992. Months would go by and he would build up his Flickr site with art and photography, and then suddenly the site would disappear from public view. Stuart (his partner) and I would beg him not to destroy it and all the wonderful comments from his admirers, but he insisted that he felt he "had to do it"—that this sacrificial act would somehow free and protect him.

He did not destroy the art itself. He knew how good it

was and called it the best work he had ever done. He preserved it carefully on external computer drives, but withdrew it from public view, perhaps irrationally fearing that even though he, the man, was well protected beyond the physical reach of any viewer, the risk of letting people see his work left him too vulnerable. Simultaneously, a large part of his personality wanted very much to be seen, to be adored, to be congratulated. What a paradoxical dilemma.

Keith told me that he had always had been extremely shy. His coping strategy was to imagine himself an actor playing the role of himself. He was quite amused with this idea. It exhilarated him to take time to "prepare" à la Method and as part of his costume he would also use makeup on his face before going out on those rare occasions when he left the house. Playing a role seemed to allow him to center himself. However, as his illness progressively left him more and more exhausted, he became less and less able to manage the tremendous swings of his internal weather. His inner resources crumbled and with that, his seclusion became his safety.

By the end of that first year, I was spending hours talking with him on Skype and gradually I began to know more of him and his life partner, Stuart Hass.

It was during these long Skype sessions that he told me he had been known as Minóy, the cassetteNoise musician. He told me the story of the 'Devil Music' Concert at Cal State Northridge. He and Phillip B. Klinger (also known as PBK) had performed a live concert at the university. They were shocked when the startling and completely unexpected response of the audience was hostility and abject fear. He had never felt so vulnerable at a performance, so hated by a crowd. Later on, in those all-too-often periods when he sank into days of despair and depression, he would relive this terrifying incident, perhaps convincing himself that his retreat into seclusion and isolation was the safest and most rational path to follow.

It was difficult for Keith to accept any kind of negative response or criticism without overreacting. He was quick to respond deeply to any slight, real or imagined, and it was almost impossible for him to brush off these feelings. They fed his paranoia and panic, and when he felt threatened and vulnerable, he retreated deeper into isolation.

Keith as Minóy disappeared completely in 1992, retreating into a hermetic-like existence with his mother and Stuart. His mother's increasingly severe mental illness added to the conjoined household burden of emotional dysfunction. He contacted no one, did not return any correspondence, and no one knew why.

Keith sent me a link to show me the last public communication of Minóy written on the outside of a package that he had sent to the musician, Zan Hofman, with whom he had been collaborating. Keith told me he'd killed off the persona of Minóy. He felt deeply betrayed and furiously angry and wanted nothing more to do with the outside world. Here is what he wrote:

> Minóy cassette works has been permanently terminated. My soul has dried up and blown away. I can no longer feel joy but only constant mental and physical (psychosomatic, so it seems) pain. We are three nonfunctional people alone in the void of Minóy house, sanctuary become prison. See and hear us go bump in the night in the day in the night in the day. It's all the same. No exit. Now we scream help.

As we now know, Keith continued to make his innovative cassette noiseMusic for a couple of years after he killed off Minóy. After Keith's death, Stuart and I felt it was important to try to preserve his work. We sent the master cassettes to Phillip B. Klinger who has digitized them for posterity. This book, as well as the accompanying cassette and CD, have been published to share some of these works with the world and to preserve the legacy of The Man Who Was Minóy.

For Keith and Stuart, the rest of the 1990s was progressively more and more arduous and frustrating.

Keith had turned his creative energies to making digital art and he renamed himself "My Life as a Haint," then "Haint." In southern United States English vernacular, a haint is a ghost, an apparition, a lost soul. Years of doctors and medication had not cured him nor had it slowed the relentless progress towards the inevitable. He knew he would never regain the health he had lost and he was consumed with grief and anger.

So often we see brilliantly creative people plagued with mental afflictions, illnesses I have come to believe have their origins in overly intense and innate sensitivities to the vicissitudes of life. The delicate neurochemistry of the brain and body goes awry and can slide into self-propagating, never-ending cascades of reaction and tortuous re-reaction twisting and turning to try to maintain stasis—to reach a mental and physical status quo.

As we reach our later years of life on this earth there is a tendency to gravitate downward as our resources for existence dwindle. Keith and Stuart were fated to experience this dwindle way too early in their lives. In the 1990s they were only in their early 40s, but the world was beginning to collapse in on them with a vengeance, drastically closing them in, isolating them.

As the years went by, Keith's fears caused them to become entirely cloistered: no family, no friends, no casual relationships with their neighbors. As he became more and more incapacitated by his physical and mental afflictions, Stuart was swept along with him into their conjoined isolation. They were cocooned in a house filled to the brim with the prodigious agglomeration of their lives, yet all of this cushioning barely mitigated Keith's profound and all-consuming terror.

Small events can become magnified in such an isolationist environment. Reality becomes warped. There was The Incident of the Wall. After a minor earthquake, a small section of a five foot cement block wall bordering one side of the house property was knocked partially askew. Keith's response was way out of proportion. He catastrophized this relatively minor event and agonized over The Wall for months. Even after it was repaired he relived it as if it had been a major disaster in his life. Was it that his web of safety, his protective shell against the world, had been breached? I think so.

On the Image Series: Minóy as Haint as King Lear

I first visited Keith and Stuart early in 2006 and would visit them a couple of times a year over the next few years. Each time, Keith was able to muster the will and energy to get out of the house in his wheelchair and the three of us went to museums and drove joyously around Los Angeles shooting continuous exposures of light paintings. Those outings were precious to Keith as they were the only times he got out of his room. He delighted in these occasions even as the herculean effort he had to exert to cope with pain took a lot out of him. We also had several indoor shoots where we took thousands of the portraits of each other, some of which can be seen on my Flickr website.[1]

As a gift to him, to try to cheer him up, I put together an imageMontage piece called "King Lear" from some of these photo sessions (http://vimeo.com/2258762). I also made "Infinity Arcade" with the intent to show his digital art work to prospective galleries (http://vimeo.com/1947808).

---

[1] See: http://www.flickr.com/photos/amsabri/sets/.

He was drawn to the idea of publicizing his work in the art world, but would invariably change his mind and withdraw from the idea, saying no, he was too sick. It is from the "King Lear" series that Joseph Nechvatal has chosen the image portfolio for this book.

By the time I met Keith and Stuart in 2005 and began to interact in their lives, their world was collapsing. Keith's mental and physical issues were ever-worsening and Stuart was breaking down. He was worn out, never getting enough sleep, sinking more deeply into the mire of his own lifelong depression, becoming more frazzled. In retrospect, we see that Stuart's incipient early dementia had already begun the insidious destruction of his brilliant mind.

There were times when Stuart would call me to help Keith calm down. I could hear Keith in full panic state, screaming and sobbing, raging, raving, ranting on and on. It would take hours for him to calm himself down. Keith in the throes of a panic attack was a formidable and disturbing thing to hear. It was scary as hell.

He did his best to deal with his daemons and had amazing powers of recuperation, but his exacerbating illnesses were increasingly impacting his mind and body and it became harder and harder to define what was Keith and what was illness.

The last dreadful half year before Keith died was filled with emergency visits from the fire department to help him get up from the floor where he had fallen and several hospitalizations. By this time all he could do was listen to music. I was able to speak a few words with him on the day he died. Stuart was with him, holding him in his arms.

I knew Keith Stanley Bowsza for the last five years of his life and I knew him as the digital artist, photographer and videographer who named himself 'My Life as A Haint.'

His spirit is one of my guardian angels, and I imagine him looking down from the cosmos, ecstatic that people will be able to enjoy his work via these publications.

The day he died
Keith said to me,
"I love you, sweetie. Stay in the light."

In Commemoration to you, my dearest Haint.

My darling Keith,
your corporeal body passed into this Earth too soon, cheating you out
of years of life.

If only there had been a magic potion to cure you of your afflictions,
if only fate had given a full lifetime to enjoy,
if only . . .

For over half your life you struggled with brainTangled cascades of
maniacal neuronScreams that rarely left you in peace.

Your death was a death that brought relief. Tragic and sorrowful
though it was, it was the only solution to ease your suffering, the
ultimate best solution in a situation where there are no good solutions.

Musings of my neonHeart . . . where it all comes from . . . the heart
and the mind
the soul the art the music the passion the love.
The world around us will forever be demented . . .
the flesh next to mine . . .
the air downtown . . . perverted strangers . . .
the blinded whiteHouse . . .
. . . the world at large enthralled with violence
pushing and steaming and
bursting to get it on get it going and roll on and rollover and
crush her human children into despair.
The light keeps us going . . . looking for the light . . .
looking for sugar . . .
looking for relief . . . looking for safety . . . looking for love.
Have no fear . . . but know when to duck . . .
when to step aside . . . when to

let darkness pass because it is blinded by hate
and it doesn't even know you
but it hates your guts and if you try to reason with it or snare it or snag
it or engage it in any possible way it will kill you in the end . . .
eat you alive . . .
so let it go . . .
stay in the light.

Stay in the light, my darling Keith, bask in the light . . .
let it caress you from the darkness
seize it from the darkness . . .
pull it towards you and don't let go.

You are safe.

Minóy as Haint as King Lear

photographs by Maya Eidolon

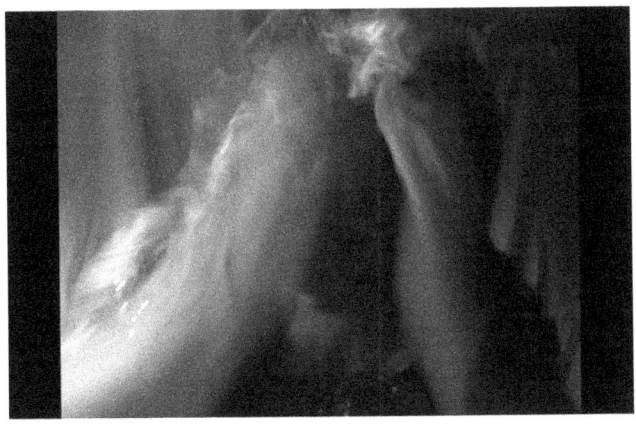

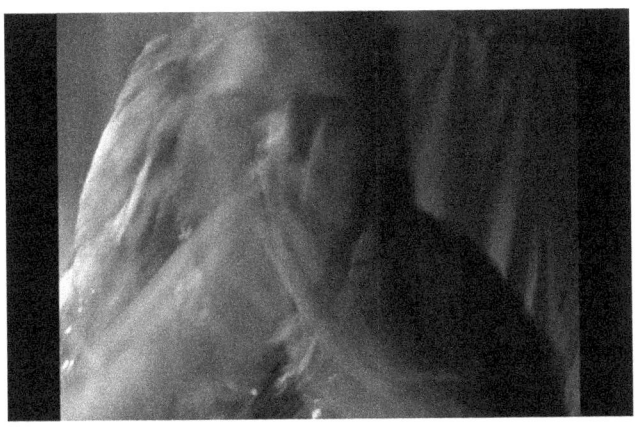

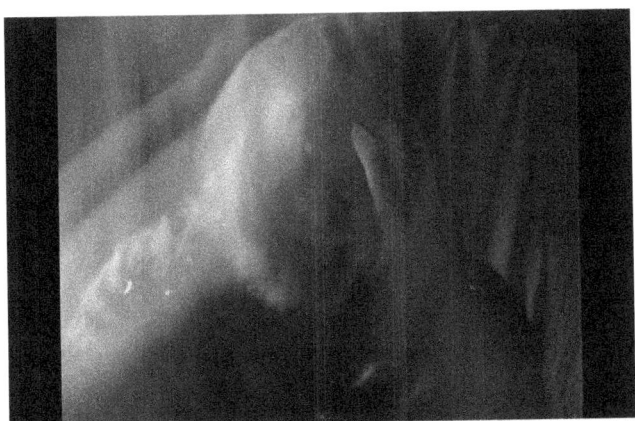

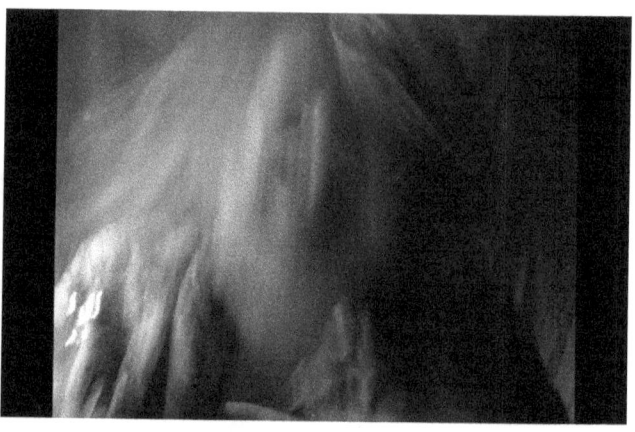

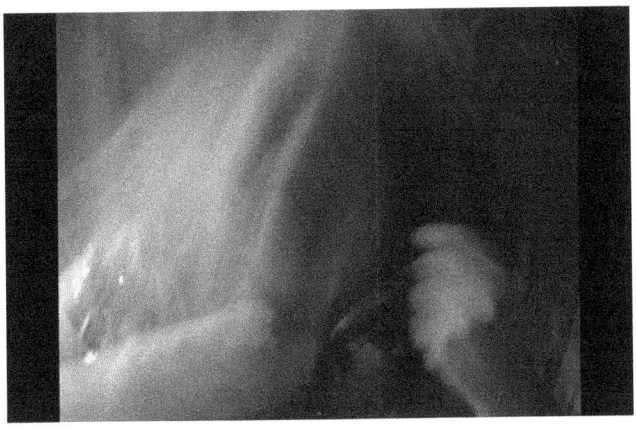

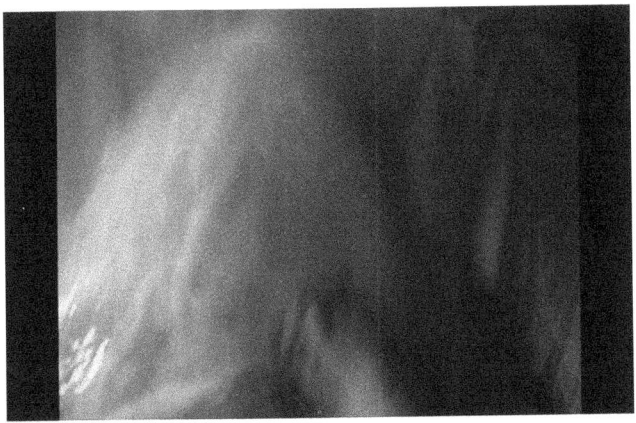

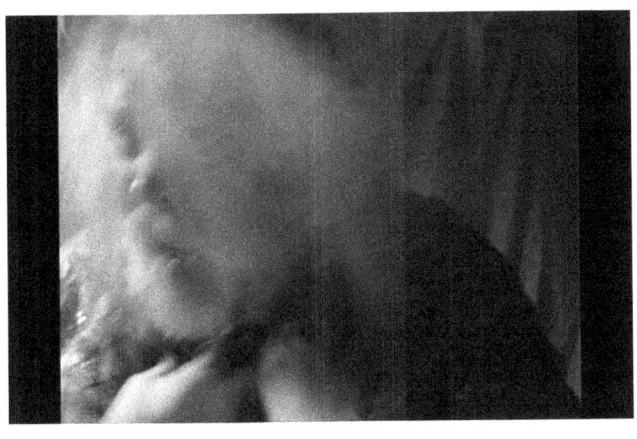

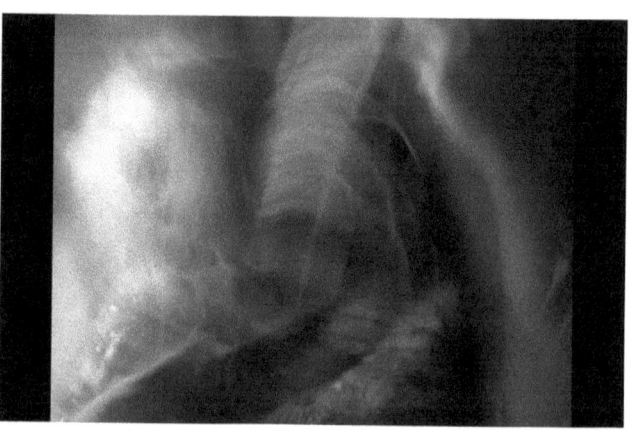

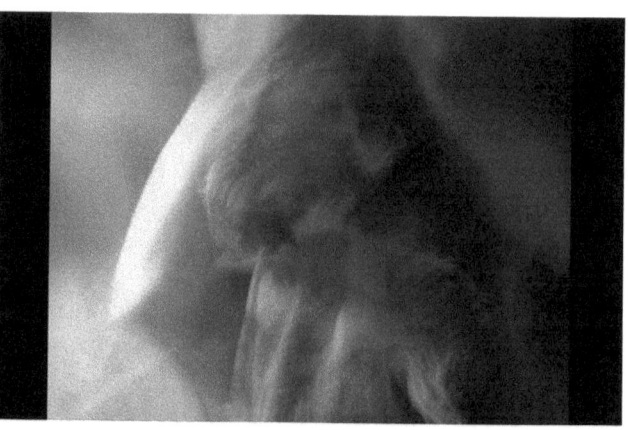

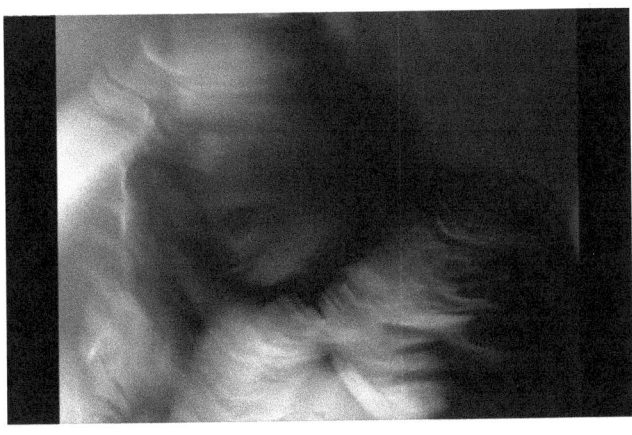

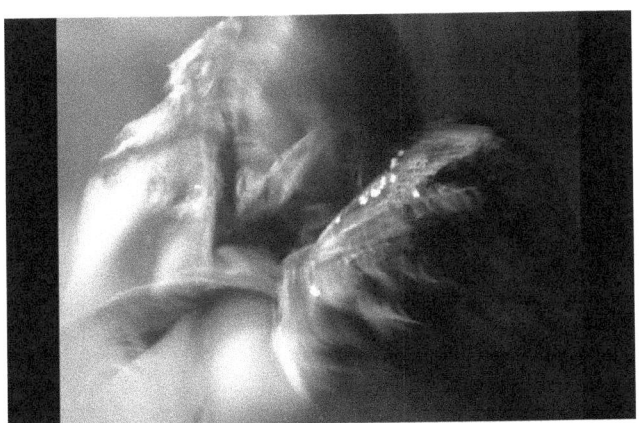

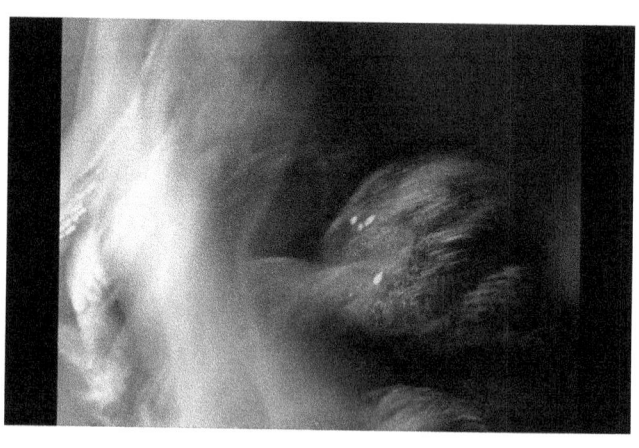

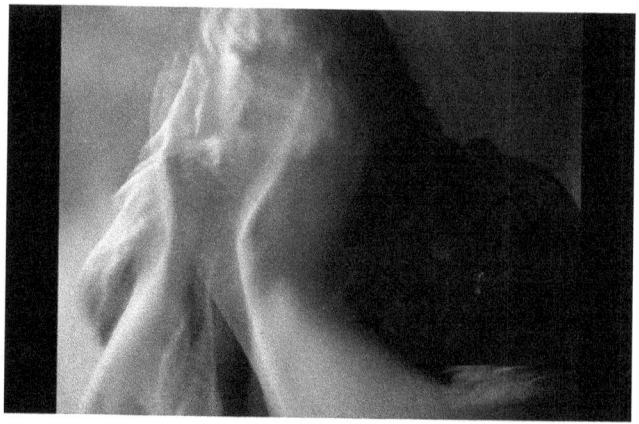

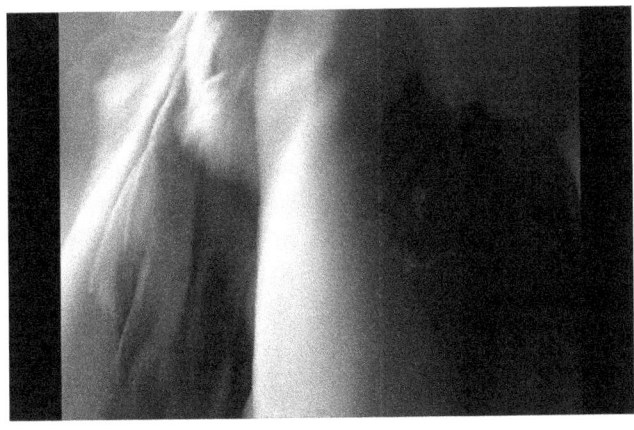

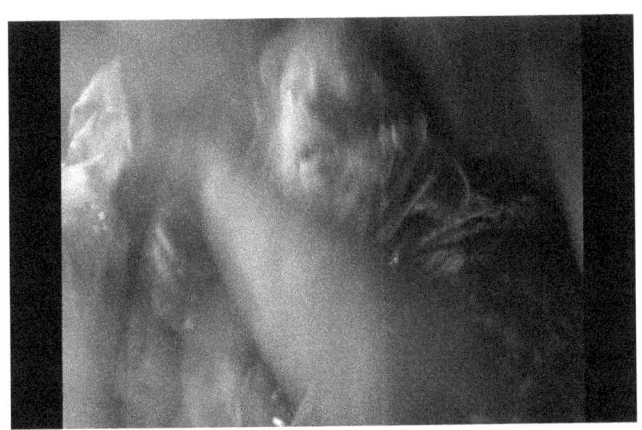

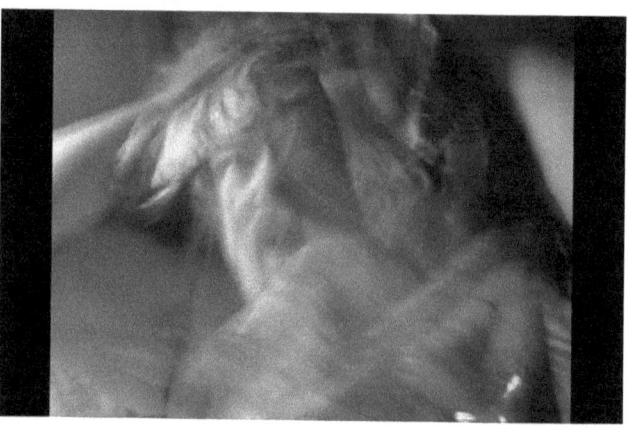

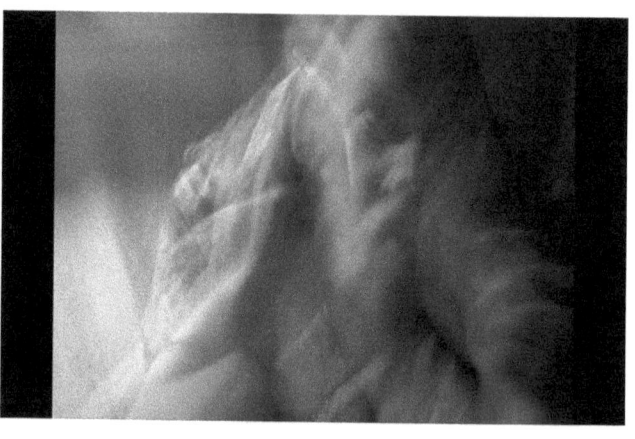

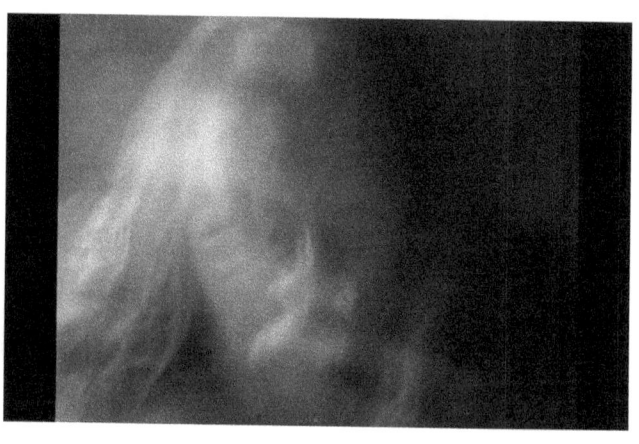

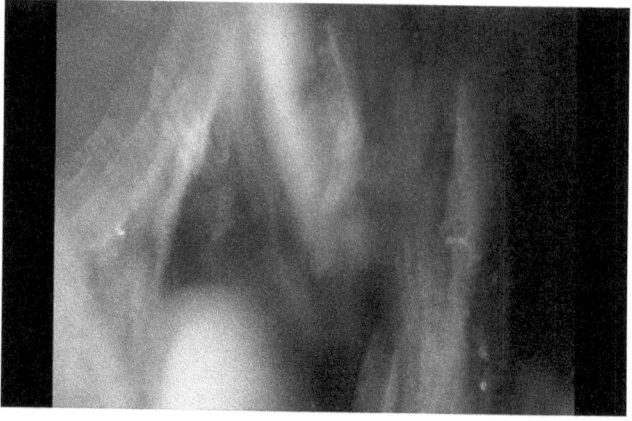

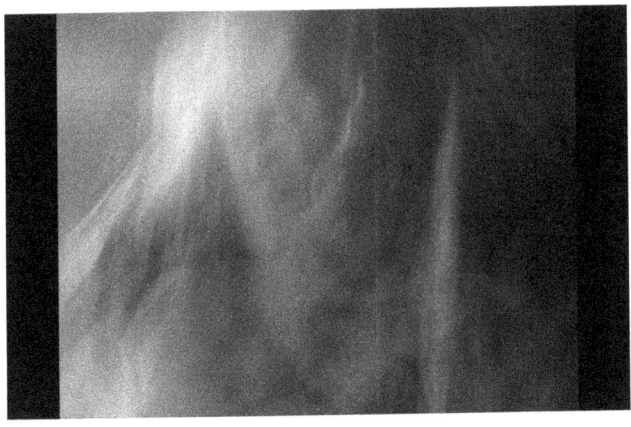

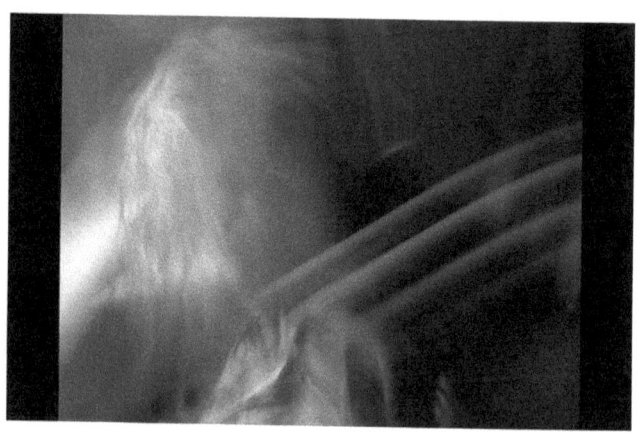

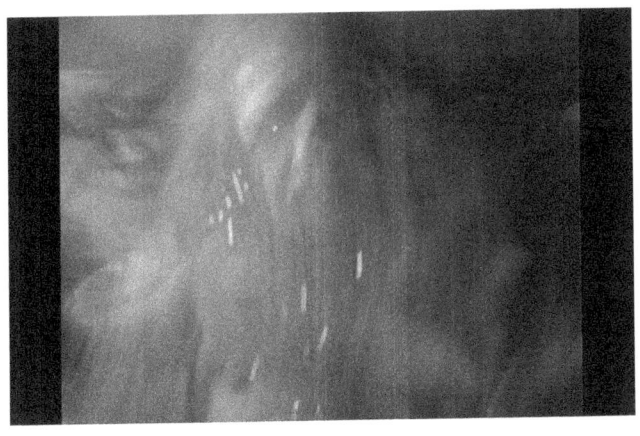

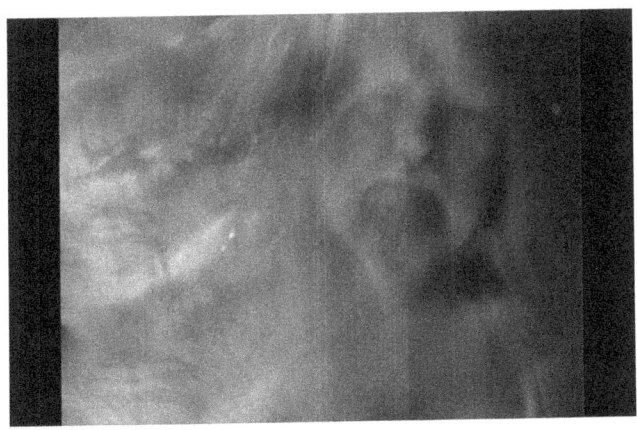

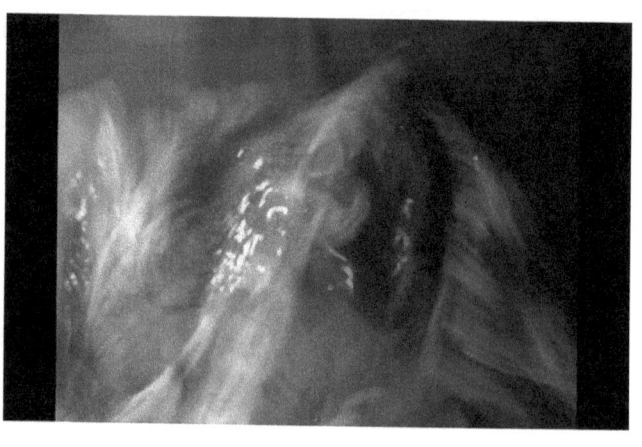

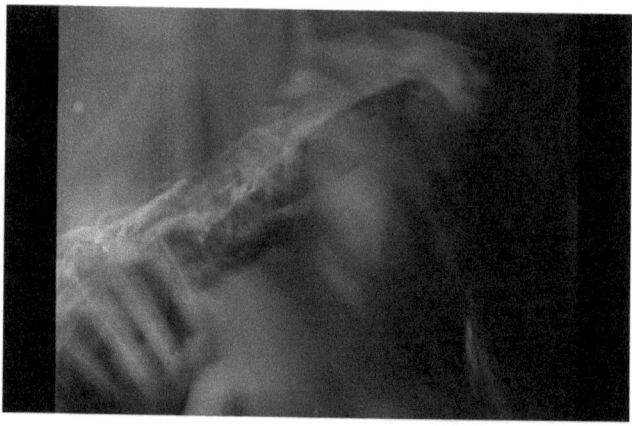

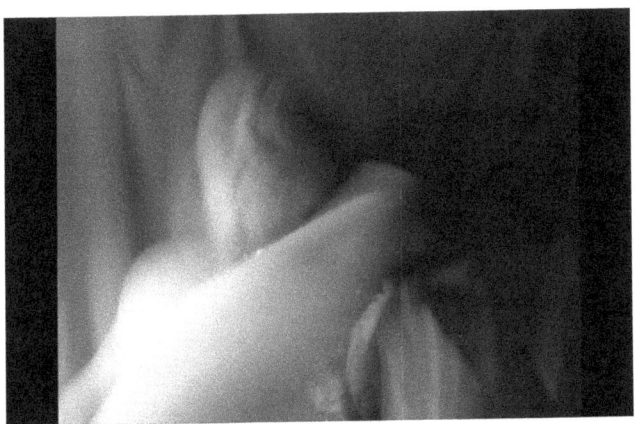

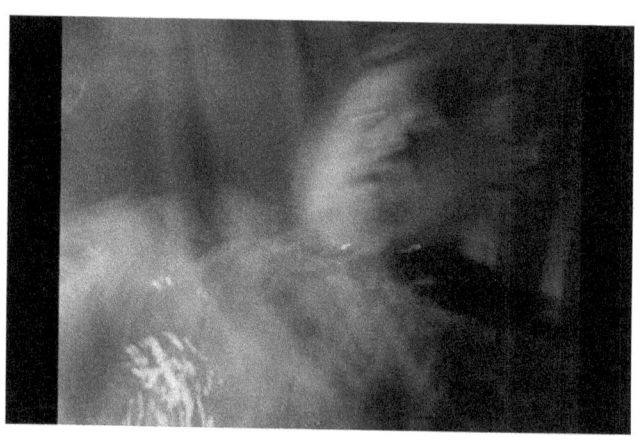

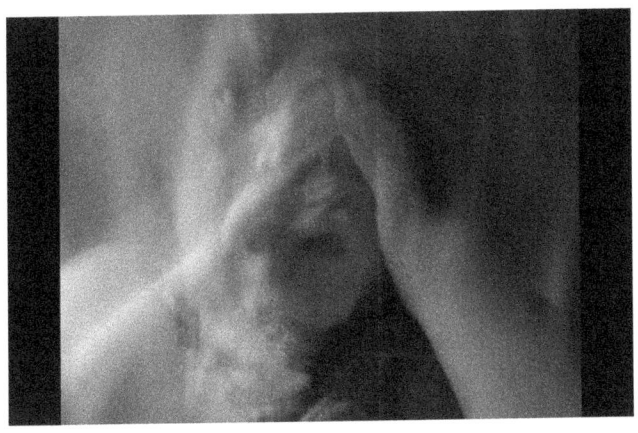

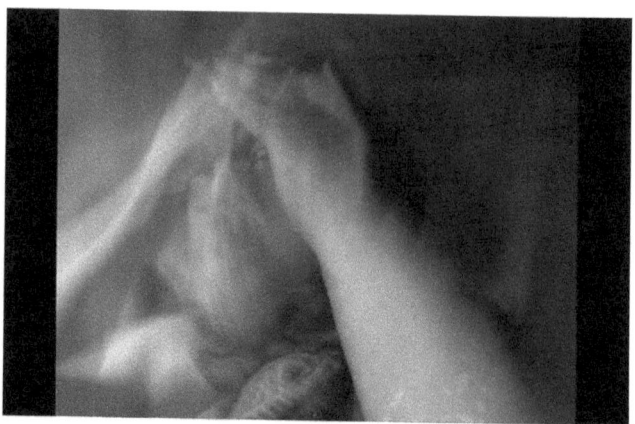

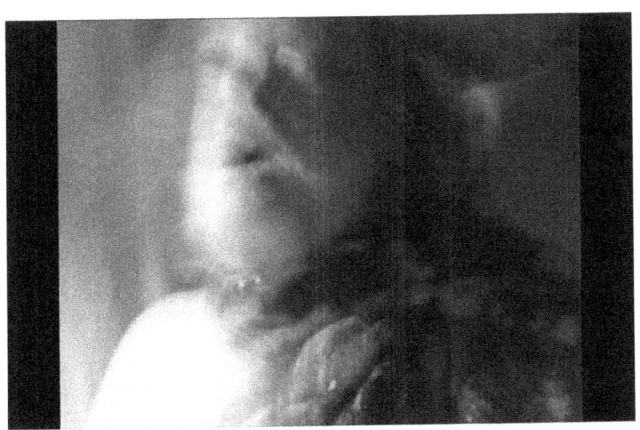

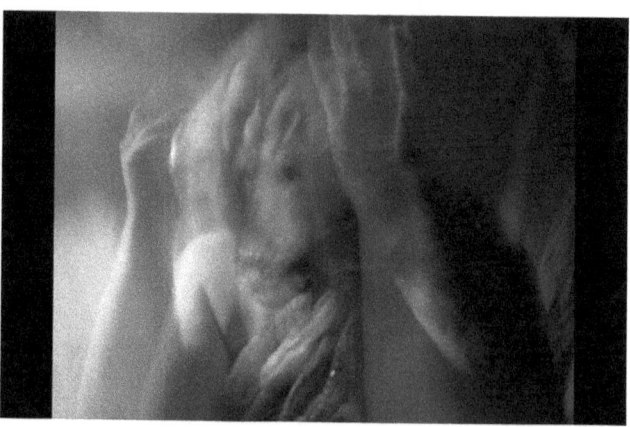

After Words

THE OBSCURITY OF MINÓY

Joseph Nechvatal

Is it so a noise to be is it a least remain to rest, is it a so old say to be, is it a leading are been. Is it so, is it so, is it so, is it so is it so is it so.
    Gertrude Stein, *Tender Buttons*

Solitude, that dread goddess and mater saeva cupidinum, encircles and besets him, ever more threatening, more violent, more heartbreaking—but who today knows what solitude is?
    Friedrich Nietzsche, *Human, All Too Human:*
    A Book for Free Spirits

But he still did not know who he was . . .
    Michael Knerr, *The Sex Life of the Gods*

He was feeling his way through obscurities.
    Aldous Huxley, *Mortal Coils*

The initiative behind this book and CD has been developed as a project to rescue Minóy from obscurity. Therefore, in the shadow of eldritch Priest's essay "Obscurity and the Poetics of Non/Sense,"[1] I would like to explain a bit of how the Minóy project emerged out of obscurity, while simultaneously promoting the aesthetics of obscurity.

In large measure, we owe a debt of gratitude to my coproducer, Phillip B. Klingler (PBK), for its existence. Phillip had known Minóy since 1987, when Minóy was at the peak of his audio creativity. Phillip had been reading reviews of his music in the cassette underground press, notably pieces in *Option* and *Sound Choice*, where critics were calling Minóy a *master of sound collage* and a *must-hear maximalist*. Phillip sent Minóy a letter and ordered some tapes from him, but nothing quite prepared him for the unique world of Minóy's music. In private correspondence, Phillip explained to me what Minóy's dense musical abstractions meant to him, and how he perceived them. He described Minóy's noise music in obscure terms, which is appropriate, as the origin of any sound in a Minóy track is most often indiscernible, thus creating an otherworldly abstract experience. Phillip found the work "dream-like, nightmare-like, but also sometimes spiritual," and Minóy's sound affected him deeply.

Phillip (a painter at the time) sent Minóy his first sound experiments—and they were met with positive, validating comments from Minóy. Consequently, they started talking on the phone frequently. They had both been involved in the mail art scene, so were already on common collaborative sharing ground. In the mid 1980s, Phillip had been exhibiting his paintings around the L.A. area, obsessed with moving deeper into abstraction. When he heard Minóy's music, he knew that the abstract possibilities with sound expression were nearly limitless—and Minóy provided an artistic model for him. Through their developing relationship (he collabo-

---

[1] eldritch Priest, "Obscurity and the Poetics of Non/Sense in the Writings of Raymond Roussel and Fernando Pessoa," *Mosaic* 45.2 (June 2012): 1–17.

rated live with Minóy in Torrance, California and worked very closely with him throughout 1987 into 1988, making something like ten albums together under different names), he discovered that Minóy would stay up for days and nights on end without sleep, very excitedly, and compulsively, creating artworks and music. After that, Minóy would spend days in bed, depressed and non-communicative.

Through this creative process, Phillip discovered that as dense as Minóy's music could often be, it was created with rather limited instrumentation: electric guitar, synthesizer, shortwave radio, and a Sony Pro Walkman. The only effects unit he used was a beloved Radio Shack spring reverb. Minóy didn't use the common four-track recorder to overdub his sounds, and instead he dubbed back and forth between several Boom Boxes and cassette recorders that he would place in different proximities around his room. Minóy would do this over and over until he had achieved the spatial audio effects he desired.

As Phillip recounted to me, 1986 was the first year Minóy obsessively documented his sound works. The results were 33 full-length albums created in a twelve-month period. This manic, compulsive need to create more and more art—where ideas flow into work after work—would typify Minóy's working method. During a fevered six-year period (between 1986 and 1992) Minóy created hundreds of cassette albums.

Minóy defined the concept of *mail collaboration*, which suited his personality and his phobias well. (As I previously mentioned, he was an agoraphobic, didn't like to travel and could not drive a car.) Minóy was addicted to his mailbox and would receive huge stacks of mail. He even adopted the name *No Mail On Sundays* for his collaborative project with Damian Bisciglia, a reference to their mutual postal addiction.

Phillip (PBK) performed live with Minóy at the University of California, San Bernardino, in 1988—a show that became scandalous. Minóy had a colorful cloth that he had draped over his head and shoulders, his nails were painted black, and one could not see his face at all. He was doing a sort of Butoh-inspired strange, slow dance, while howling some anguished mashup of *Somewhere Over The Rainbow* and, ironically, *I Get By (With A Little Help From My Friends)*. Campus crusaders shut the concert down, turning the sound system off after only fifteen minutes onstage, but the noise music continued for an hour, played through their own amps. This has been documented with a tape called *Devil Music: Minóy Live* (cassette released on the *Nihilistic Recordings* label in Holland).[2] The press clearly loved the scandal (no surprise there), but events like this made Minóy acutely aware of how unacceptable and misunderstood his creative works were by society at large—how obscure he really was.

This concert led to a dissipation of PBK's and Minóy's creative energies in collaboration, and they never worked together again. Phillip didn't correspond with Minóy after that, but he was aware of Minóy's activities in the noise underground. Their solo works appeared together on many tape compilations from that time.

When Phillip came online around 2000, it was basically known amongst mutual friends that Minóy had dropped out and was not making music any more, and he had also completely stopped corresponding with his music friends. It has now become known that it was in 1992 that Minóy wrote to a close collaborator, Zan Hoffman, informing him that *Minóy Cassetteworks* (his DIY label) was over, writing (as Amber Sabri shares in her memoir in this volume),

> Minóy Cassetteworks has been permanently terminated.

---

[2] This recording, as a digital file, and more information on the concert and its reception, has been uploaded by Hal McGee to http://archive.org/details/DevilMusicMinoyLive.

> My soul has dried up and blown away. I can no longer feel joy but only constant mental and physical (psychosomatic, so it seems) pain. We are three non-functioning people alone in the void of the Minóy house, sanctuary become prison. See and hear us go bump in the night in the day in the night in the day. It's all the same. No exit. Now we scream help.

After 1992, nothing else was heard of (or from) Minóy.

In 2012, Phillip started doing some intense internet research and came upon a posting that Minóy's partner, Stuart Haas, had made on an obscure mail-art site. It said Minóy had died in 2010. With Minóy's old house address, Phillip was able to get the phone number and he called it. Stuart picked up and they talked as easily as if twenty years had not passed. Stuart told him about the sudden illness that had taken Minóy's life.

Having learned all of this within a few hours, Phillip became very concerned about the master tapes: did Stuart still have the tapes? Stuart said, "no, we threw all those out." Phillip hung up, with only Stuart's email address in hand, but following up by email proved more encouraging as Stuart later recanted, stating that he had kept any tapes that Minóy had written *master* on. Phillip was elated and wanted to help. He suggested helping digitize and archive the Minóy tape collection, yet didn't hear back from Stuart on this for quite some time. Eventually, Minóy and Stuart's good friend, Amber Sabri, stepped in to help. Amazingly, she had the complete collection of tapes Stuart had saved.

In June 2013, Phillip received three large boxes via UPS. Opening those boxes, for Phillip, was like finding the Holy Grail. In the boxes were all (or all of what was left) of Minóy's master tapes: his life in music, his legacy, everything that the man obsessed over and the things that made him famous in the 1980s cassette network.

The first thing Phillip did was physically count and document every tape in those boxes. There were at least twenty-five *lost works*: just the jewel-case/insert with titles and credits, but no tape inside. There were a number of cassettes with no written documentation on them at all. Some masters were missing completely, as there are tapes listed on the Discogs website[3] that were not found in the archive. Using all that information, Phillip was able to compile the definitive Minóy discography—and it totals 208 releases.

Because of all the mystery behind Minóy's self-imposed exile, the boxes settled a lot of questions about Minóy's creative output, especially the late period works. Still prolific in 1991, he completed almost fifty full-length albums. In 1992 there were a little over twenty, six in 1993, and in 1994 only one was found. It was the late period works that were most interesting to us for this project, as the fact that anything after 1992 even exists was extremely fascinating.

Amber Sabri related to Phillip how Minóy's parents had moved into his house (actually into the large three-car garage) and had brought all their worldly belongings with them, so now with his parents there, plus Stuart, it might have been very difficult for him to feel comfortable creating his music, even as his parents enjoyed and admired his art and music. Amber describes it as a "happy and functioning situation for all four of them. Stuart worked full-time as an aerospace engineer and the parents took over the household chores." But for whatever reason, Minóy's eerie vocalizations disappear in these last recordings.

But why did he stop all together in 1994? It may have been in part the changing technology—away from cassette to digital formats (like the CD)—that was furiously happening at that time. But Amber tells me that she believes Minóy at this moment was disenchanted with making music altogether, that he felt betrayed by certain noise musicians, and that he really meant it when he said he was finished

---

[3] See "Minóy Discography," *Discogs.com*, http://www.discogs.com/artist/84413-Minoy.

with the world as a musician. As his illnesses worsened (exacerbated by thirty years of medication treating his pain, panic, mania and paranoia, plus his morbid obesity), the creation of sound art consumed too much of his energy. He became physically less able to create anything in any form that required physical movement. As Amber recalls, Minóy's father died in early 1991 and his mother's paranoid schizophrenia became impossible to handle at home so they moved her into an assisted living facility. Minóy steadily became more and more ill and Stuart became more and more overwhelmed with working full-time, caring for him full-time, and trying to maintain all the duties of a household. It was at this point that Minóy—now calling himself Haint—turned to making digital art from within his bed.

As Phillip expressed to me, Minóy's late works seem very stern, with an angry edge to them, "ponderous structures, with sounds buzzing around, moving in little ways within a confined space, they are claustrophobic"—and that makes sense, given his situation.

For this project (this volume you now hold in your hands, or are reading on-screen, plus the cassette and CD released from punctum records titled, simply, *Minóy*), Phillip combed through the archive in search of shorter compositions that would represent the oeuvre. This was a challenge, as the vast majority of Minóy's compositions are of running time between thirty to forty-five minutes in length. As Phillip articulated to me:

> Listening to Minóy's music is sort of like watching a movie: it takes you on a journey, the twists and turns can't be anticipated because nothing repeats, the structure is always in flux until it ends. The sounds aren't literal. They're metaphoric only in the most abstract way. These long, elaborate pieces were essential to Minóy's aesthetic of a *cinema of the ear*, allowing him to explore outside of time restrictions that would apply to avant-garde sound artists working in the shorter LP format.

Yet Phillip and I were not interested in editing longer compositions down to excerpts for this project. We were more interested in compiling a collection of his shorter works from different time-frames in his career, thus allowing a listener to come away with a greater sense of Minóy's achievements, and thus also the bigger picture of what Phillip calls his "musical genius."

After After Words

THE AESTHETICS OF AN OBSCURE MONSTER SACRÉ

Joseph Nechvatal

In the beginning was the noise.
                    Michele Serres, *The Parasite*

Recently in my book *Immersion Into Noise*[1] I mapped out a broad-spectrum of aesthetic activity I call the *art of noise* by tracing its past eruptions where figure/ground merge and flip the common emphasis to some extent. *Immersion Into Noise* concludes with a look at the figural aspect of this aesthetic lodged within the ground of consciousness itself.[2] For

---

[1] Joseph Nechvatal, *Immersion Into Noise* (Ann Arbor: Open Humanities Press/MPublishing, 2011).
[2] This involves a question of the qualities (and levels) of awareness of our own consciousness within aesthetic realms which we are capable of attaining through noise art.

me, the obscurity of Minóy exemplifies well a general noise aesthetic needed now within our broad-spectrum data-monitoring info-economy environment of background machine-to-machine gigabyte communication murmur[3] in which we now find ourselves. Minóy is a good example of the speculative reality of noise music aesthetics[4] in our era of algorithmic globalization.

This reflection on Minóy is somewhat of a reaction to what some interesting contemporary philosophers have been saying about contemporary art. Most notably, the surprising talk "The Next Avant-Garde" that the philosopher Graham Harman gave at the *Aesthetics in the 21st Century* conference at the University of Basel in September 2012, which engaged me with the recent *speculative realism*[5] turn in conti-

---

[3] Stupendous amounts of data generated by nearly one billion people are set in motion each day as, with an innocuous click or tap, people download movies on iTunes, check credit card balances through Visa's website, send e-mail with files attached, buy products, post on Twitter, or read newspapers and art theory papers online.

[4] Noise Music in general traffics in dissonance, atonality, distortion, incidental composing, etc. This music begins with Luigi Russolo's *reti di rumori* (networks of noises) music that he performed on his intonarumori noise instuments and with his text "The Art of Noises: Futurist Manifesto," in Christoph Cox and Daniel Warner, eds., *Audio Culture: Readings in Modern Music* (London: Continuum, 2004). For more of the history of noise music, see Paul Hegarty, *Noise/Music: A History* (New York: Continuum, 2007) and Nechvatal, *Immersion Into Noise*, 39–47.

[5] Speculative realism is a movement in contemporary philosophy which defines itself loosely in its stance of anti-correlationist metaphysical realism against the dominant forms of post-Kantian philosophy or what it terms correlationism (meaning philosophies that apprehend being and the world via human-centered lenses, where any understanding of being and the world is always correlated to what it means *for* or *to* humans, or how insight into being and the world looks, feels, etc., is shaped according to

nental philosophy and aesthetics. In that talk Harman criticizes Relational Art,[6] calling it convivial art, so as to circle back to the formalist, media-specific aesthetics of the art critic Clement Greenberg, where art objects are free of the "tyranny of context." This supposed context freedom merges efficiently with Harman's theory of Object Oriented Ontology (OOO),[7] but seemed somewhat at odds with his proclaiming that "there must be a new avant-garde in every field" that we cannot predict. His return to the formalist, media specific aesthetics is hard to swallow in terms of avant-garde ideals.

Harman then touched on the subject of figure/ground relations (the main focus of my own noise art aesthetic theory) in terms of anthropomorphic free, flat ontology

---

human perspectives). While often in disagreement over basic philosophical issues, the speculative realist thinkers (such as Harman, Ray Brassier, and Quentin Meillassoux, among others) have a shared resistance to philosophies of human finitude inspired by the tradition of Immanuel Kant.

[6] Relational art or relational aesthetics is a mode or tendency in fine art practice originally observed and highlighted by French art critic Nicolas Bourriaud. Bourriaud defined the approach simply as a set of artistic practices which take as their theoretical and practical point of departure the whole of human relations and their social context, rather than an independent and private space. The artist can be more accurately viewed as the "catalyst" in relational art, rather than being at the center.

[7] Object Oriented Ontology (OOO) is a metaphysical movement that rejects the privileging of human existence over the existence of nonhuman objects. Specifically, OOO opposes the anthropocentrism of Immanuel Kant's Copernican Revolution, whereby objects are said to conform to the mind of the subject and, in turn, become products of human cognition. In contrast to Kant's view, object-oriented philosophers maintain that objects exist independently of human perception and are not ontologically exhausted by their relations with humans or other objects.

without going very far in addressing the human specialness[8] (relationality) involved in viewing certain artworks. I mentioned to Harman, à propos, the irony of the intense dislike that Greenberg had for the late last work of Jackson Pollock, when Pollock went semi-representational, playing with indeterminate states of figure/ground ambiguity—for example, Jackson Pollock's portrait of Jane Smith, *No. 7* (1952), that I saw numerous times at her home, now owned by the Metropolitan Museum of Art. In his talk, Harman touched on the subject of figure/ground relations in the context of the anthropomorphic-free, flat ontology that emerged as part of the debates within the Speculative Realism movement. He coupled this figure/ground discussion with a Greenbergian medium-specific version of the Object-Oriented Ontology defense of an ontology of objects (rather than processes). This was a welcome tonic in a relationally committed, but miserable, Europe of depressed post-convergent labor. I found remarkable his defense of objects amid the soaring (some would say souring) contemporary art trend of relations (de-aesthetized and dematerialized). Yet Harman failed to adequately account for the human singular (non-anthropomorphic-free) aspect involved in experiencing the art of noise, with its reversals in the order of figure/ground.

Without a rethinking of human singularity, I suggest that this omission conceals a concern for relational power, as we know from the life of Clement Greenberg. With the officially sanctioned support[9] and celebration of relational dematerialization (celeb-commodified into a brand – and co-opted by the star-state-socio-economic system that is its

---

[8] Art's coherence stems from human values and symbolic systems and the role of the beholder, and thus is, and must be, correlational and anthropocentric.

[9] Curators promoting this "laboratory" paradigm include Maria Lind, Hans Ulrich Obrist, Barbara van der Linden, Hou Hanru, and Nicolas Bourriaud.

life blood) the relational aesthetic[10] is no longer an idealized mode of art activity that (supposedly) accepts the full range of all human relations as art in opposition to private objects and spaces. That has petered out, found now often unsympathetically aloof: afloat within relational administrative systems of power.[11] The ideal of artistic exploration[12] of the full range of *all* human relations is clearly untenable at this administrative level—and obscure, singular human intimacy pays the price. The relational artist as catalyst[13]—by means of flighty creations of intentionally stuplime[14] works that fluctuate between sculpture, music, film clips and small Fluxus-like events—has turned the artist into a star-impresario-entrepreneur: a very specific, limiting and quasi-domineering human relation. Coupled with fun-house-laboratory work based in an aesthetic paradigm of aloofness that is so

---

[10] Established by Nicolas Bourriaud, now director of the École Nationale Supérieure des Beaux-Arts in Paris.

[11] 2013 examples include Philippe Parreno's *Anywhere, anywhere out of the* world at the Palais de Tokyo, Pierre Huyghe's retrospective at Le Centre Pompidou, The Dia Art Foundation-sponsored *Gramsci Monument* by Thomas Hirschhorn, and Tino Sehgal's win of the Golden Lion for the best artist in the *International Exhibition Il Palazzo Enciclopedico* in the Venice Biennale.

[12] Artists included by Bourriaud under the rubric of Relational Aesthetics include Rirkrit Tiravanija, Philippe Parreno, Carsten Höller, Henry Bond, Douglas Gordon and Pierre Huyghe, among others.

[13] See "The Menagerie Entertains," my review of the Pierre Huyghe Retrospective at Le Centre Pompidou in *The Brooklyn Rail*, December 18, 2013: http://www.brooklynrail.org/2013/12/artseen/pierre-huyghe-the-menagerie-entertains.

[14] In Chapter 6, "Stuplimity," of her book *Ugly Feelings* (Cambridge, MA: Harvard University Press, 2005), Sianne Ngai offers this term as a necessary reaction to new, primarily postmodern objects of analysis, a term that acknowledges stupidity and boredom as part of the sublime expression connected to the postmodern art experience.

cool it verges on cold, the relational art star is placed firmly back at the top-center of things and torn *away* from art that creates a social environment in which people come together to participate in a private-but-shared activity that is open-ended, interactive and resistant to closure.

I would make the case for a return to the art object as post-conceptually scalable and mutable (as opposed to art as process alone) that owes something to Harman's OOO object (stopping short of his context freeness) because the inherent detachment of work-in-progress post-medium practice, shorn of any deep commitment to medium specificity, seems to inscribe a limiting condition of superficiality on the artist while bestowing media success—a truly Mephistopheles-like metaphysical situation that, as Claire Bishop has suggested, "seems to derive from a creative misreading of poststructuralist theory: rather than the interpretations of a work of art being open to continual reassessment, the work of art itself is argued to be in perpetual flux."[15]

Also, I have been following closely the public proclamations of another philosopher on art, Simon Critchley. Critchley described in 2010 contemporary art's dominant trend as an in-authenticity of "mannerist situationism" based in rituals of reenactment.[16] Critchley goes on in 2012 to describe the circumstances further, as the "cold mannerist obsessionality of the taste for appropriation and reenactment that has become hegemonic in the art world."[17] So things

---

[15] Claire Bishop, "Antagonism and Relational Aesthetics," *October* 110 (Fall 2004): 52.

[16] Simon Critchley, "The Faith of the Faithless: Experiments in Political Theology," Dance Politics & Co-Immunity Workshop, Giessen, Germany, November 12, 2010. See also Simon Critchley, *The Faith of the Faithless: Experiments in Political Theology* (London: Verso, 2014).

[17] Simon Critchley, "Absolutely-Too-Much," *The Brooklyn Rail*, August 1, 2012: http://www.brooklynrail.org/2012/08/art/absolutely-too-much.

have gotten no better. Clearly something deep-seated must be reevaluated. And art aesthetics is more interesting when it does the work of shifting meaning. So I am declining here Critchley's urging for contemporary art to focus in on the *monstrous*, as, in my opinion, that parody of gloomy general dystopia only plays into the extreme spectacle aspect of mannerism. To be fair, Critchley doesn't explain what or who he means by the monstrous, but when I think of the monstrous today I think of the high visibility of Lady Gaga (and her little monsters), extreme Hollywood lowbrow movies, and grotesque far right political claims and postures.

No, here I am only interested in a new contemporary aesthetic labor based in a certain exquisite untouchability, and unseeablity—Minóy's obscure *monster sacré* affinity of disconnectedness, which focuses on an impregnable diva-like commitment to a nihilistic aesthetic of *becoming imperceptible*[18] (á la Ad Reinhardt blackness, but one that takes you into embodied and embedded resonance perspectives, into radical immanence, and away from extreme pure abstractions). I am interested in an exquisite *monster sacré* aesthetic for Minóy (where personal anthropomorphic eccentricities and indiscretions are tolerated) that is bent on combining the neo-materialist[19] vibrant world with a wider vis-

---

[18] "Although all becomings are already molecular, including becoming woman, it must be said that all becomings begin with and pass through becoming-woman. It is the key to all the other becomings. . . . If becoming-woman is the first quantum, or molecular segment, with the becomings-animal that link up with it coming next, what are they all rushing toward? Without a doubt, toward *becoming-imperceptible*. The imperceptible is the immanent end of becoming, its cosmic formula": Gilles Deleuze and Félix Guattari, *A Thousand Plateaus: Capitalism and Schizophrenia*, trans. Brian Massumi (Minneapolis: University of Minnesota Press, 1987), 279.

[19] Manuel DeLanda coined the term "neo-materialist" in a short 1996 text, "The Geology of Morals: A Neo-Materialist Inter-

ion of political awareness including private spiritual, ecstatic or numinous themes accessible through the generative subjective realm of each individual; an aesthetics of perception-politics based on resonance (not a politics of visibility) which reveals in minute particulars the full spectrum of the extensive social-political dimension.

This *monster sacré* affinity is a materialist nihilism of *no* that (if it goes far enough) can transform a metamorphosis (subject to the flickering formative forces of emergence)[20] into an all-embracing *yes* of delicate abhorrence.[21] So I am advocating here not the passive and thus incomplete nihilism of form, but a generative and virulent and curative nihilism that unleashes forces of reverberation to emerge and resonate like a web of inter-connected, molecular and viral relational affects and intensities that traffics in dissonance, deviation, and the incidental.

But what specifically can we glean for art from this instability and resonance of covert nihilism? In what kind of regimes of attraction/repulsion can the resonant nihilistic art object participate, and what may it do differently from other signs and objects? To these questions I offer a counter-theory to OOO's formalism, a theory of *à rebours*[22] ex-

---

pretation," *Virtual Futures* 95 (1995), where he treats a portion of Deleuze and Guattari's *A Thousand Plateaus* in order to conceptualize geological movements. For more on neo-materialism, see Manuel DeLanda's interview in *New Materialism: Interviews & Cartographies*, eds. Rick Dolphijn and Iris van der Tuin (Ann Arbor: Open Humanities Press/ MPublishing, 2012), 38.

[20] In philosophy, systems theory, science, and art, emergence is the way complex systems and patterns arise out of a multiplicity of relatively simple interactions. Emergence is central to the theories of integrative levels and of complex systems.

[21] For a musical comparison, see "The Beauty of Noise: An Interview with Masami Akita of Merzbow," in Cox and Warner, eds., *Audio Culture: Readings in Modern Music*, 59–61.

[22] The meaning of *à rebours* is against the grain. Also, *À rebours*

changes of figure/ground relationships: a nimble art that emphasizes human and non-human entanglements. This is an art that depends on playing out nihilistic negativity by intensifying its forces into an affirmative nihilism. This nimble nihilist bracketing pushes the audience towards open defamiliarizations, challenging them to think outside of the normal system of human consciousness. In this way it is favorable to OOO aesthetics. So this art as nimble *monster sacré* is implicated in the very type of problematic instability that the "self" undergoes in Nietzsche's thought: the cohesiveness of the culture/state distinction, like the cohesiveness of the self/other distinction, disintegrates with the ontological instability produced by the annihilation of the real as distinguishable from the illusory. With a nimble art of noise—based in the distinction between active nihilism and passive nihilism (or monstrous nihilism)—we can depict the underground vigor of form as an active verve that can only be speculated upon by thinking beyond the discursive.

The embeddedness of our inner world—the life of our imagination with its intense drives, suspicions, fears, and loves—guides our intentions and actions in the political-economic world. Our inner world is the only true source of meaning and purpose we have and nimble exquisite gazing[23] (that involves self-investigation) is the way to discover for ourselves this inner life. So we might consider now that, in contrast to our frenzied data market surveillance culture,[24]

(1884) (translated as *Against Nature* or *Against the Grain*) is a decadent novel by the French writer Joris-Karl Huysmans. Its narrative concentrates on the tastes and inner life of Jean Des Esseintes, an eccentric, reclusive aesthete and antihero who loathes bourgeois society and tries to retreat into an ideal artistic world of his own creation.

[23] *Gaze*: to look long and intently. *Gaze* is often indicative of wonder, fascination, and revelation.

[24] For example, take the blandly named Utah Data Center, National Security Agency. A project of once immense secrecy, it is

that which trains us to fear the atrocious eyes of outer perception, a protracted and absorbing gazing art (like Minóy's) could encourage the development of agile clandestine exchanges based on the embedded individual intuitive eye in conjunctive contact with an abundant *optical-mnemonic commons* (not cloud)[25] that shares a sensibility for building a force. What I mean by optical-mnemonic commons is a visual memory of possible shared futures, a mnemonic gazing at that intersubjective affinity that we share as the cooperative common ground of sociality: that shared common ground that precedes community. Such a commons of exchange is what has to be built politically through the creation of innovative individual-polis assemblages; new modes of organization of the individual-collective from which all could benefit.

Of course this sphere of anti-purist gazing-commons (essentially a cooperative rejection of the tyranny of labels,

---

the final piece in a complex puzzle assembled over the past decade. Its purpose: to intercept, decipher, analyze, and store vast swaths of the world's communications as they zap down from satellites and zip through the underground and undersea cables of international, foreign, and domestic networks. Flowing through its servers and routers and stored in near-bottomless databases are all forms of communication, including the complete contents of private e-mails, cell phone calls, and Google searches, as well as all sorts of personal data trails—parking receipts, travel itineraries, bookstore purchases, and other digital transactions. It is, in some measure, the realization of the "total information awareness" program created during the first term of the Bush administration—an effort that was killed by Congress in 2003 after it caused an outcry over its potential for invading Americans' privacy. For more on this trend, see James Bamford, *The Shadow Factory: the Ultra-Secret NSA from 9/11 to the Eavesdropping on America* (New York: Anchor Books, 2009).

[25] The term "cloud" is generally used to describe a data center's functions. More specifically, it refers to a service for leasing computing capacity.

essential identities, privileged abstractions, and fixed ideas) is what allows art to construct unstable distinctions between subjects and objects that embrace the entire spectrum of imaginary spaces—from the infinitude of actual forms to formless voids of virtuality. Subsequently my interest here is in anti-pure nimble artists like Minóy who challenge and sometimes exchange the hierarchy of figure and ground (figure and abstraction) through struggles with noise.

Certainly globalization is all about world space, so noise art aesthetics here will continue to be thought of in terms of spatialization: dimensions, areas, and territories. What space does noise clear and what space does noise clog? How does noise function as an attractor for a gazing-commons and as a repellent in the monstrous era of global data mining and the digital surveillance state? How can *monster sacré* aesthetic thought help us to think and live differently within our smooth and surveyed spaces through art? How can we live more intently and intensely in our imaginary cosmos of pleasure rooted in the non-closure of a gazing-commons aesthetic, with its yearning for otherness in the non-appropriative mode? By not ignoring the differences between the personal and the political, but on the contrary, by showing how these differences resonate together in unpredictable and contingent ways to form, in the words of Gilles Deleuze,[26]

---

[26] Gilles Deleuze (1925-1995) was one of the most influential and prolific French philosophers of the second half of the twentieth century. Deleuze conceived of philosophy as the production of concepts, and he characterized himself as a "pure metaphysician." In his magnum opus *Difference and Repetition*, he tries to develop a metaphysics adequate to contemporary mathematics and science—a metaphysics in which the concept of multiplicity replaces that of substance, event replaces essence, and virtuality replaces possibility. Deleuze also produced studies in the history of philosophy (on Hume, Nietzsche, Kant, Bergson, Spinoza, Foucault, and Leibniz), and on the arts (a two-volume study of the cinema, books on Proust and Sacher-Masoch, a work on the painter Francis Bacon,

planes of consistency from which new political concepts can be formed.

So what does the brand *contemporary art* presently suggest for a gazing-common aesthetic? Not much, yet. Julian Stallabrass argues[27] that behind contemporary art's multiplicity and apparent capriciousness lies a monstrous bleak uniformity and that this amounts to making culture uncurious, timid, and stupid in the service of a big business ethos of unquestioning consumer conformity. Also, Stallabrass purports that the unregulated insular contemporary art market seeks to dupe newbie art rubes into being enthusiastic participants in the dumbing-down values useful to big business—values which address all communications to the lowest common denominator of the monstrously massive. So, the obvious question is: what about art's responsibility of resistance? Perhaps surprisingly, for me the answer is to be found within the challenge of a noise style based in resistance through the cultivation of invisibility.[28] So I want to argue for an agony of style of logo invisibility, and the importance that should be given within noise art aesthetic

---

and a collection of essays on literature.) Deleuze considered these latter works as pure philosophy, and not criticism, since he sought to create the concepts that correspond to the artistic practices of painters, filmmakers, and writers. In 1968, he met Félix Guattari, a political activist and radical psychoanalyst, with whom he wrote several works, among them the two-volume *Capitalism and Schizophrenia*, comprised of *Anti-Oedipus* (1972) and *A Thousand Plateaus* (1980). Their final collaboration was *What is Philosophy?* (1991).

[27] See Julian Stallabrass, *Contemporary Art: A Very Short Introduction* (Oxford, UK: Oxford University Press, 2006).

[28] Perhaps this should not be surprising given that the hidden complexity of a basic internet transaction is a mystery to most users: Sending a message with photographs to a neighbor could involve a trip through hundreds or thousands of miles of Internet conduits and multiple data centers before the e-mail arrives across the street.

struggles for a gazing-commons.

The principle of constructing patterns of infinite becomings is perhaps inherent in avant-garde artistic tradition (avant-garde values). Graham Harman suggested as much. But this avant-garde now, I think, should be considered in terms of noisy invisibility not ontology, as deviating from the regularities of visible normality provides the avant-garde new sources for artistic production. Certainly, the values of the avant-garde have always been interfering with the channels of artistic production and reception, and these values are responsible for expanding the forms and definitions of art itself.[29] But like in nature, noise in art plays a productive role in the invisible life of a system when it stresses becoming-imperceptible.

But a becoming-imperceptible-invisibile *monster sacré*, today can no longer be a form of *enfant terrible* withdrawl, akin to Marcel Duchamp's strategic invisibility,[30] but rather a phantasmagorical plunge into what Félix Guattari expresses as the *chaosmosis*.[31] In that sense, Minóy's becoming-imperceptibly noisy is an event for which there is no immediate representation.

---

[29] For more on this, read my essay "Viractuality in the Webbed Digital Age," *M/E/A/N/I/N/G Online* #5, 25th Anniversary Edition (2011): http://writing.upenn.edu/pepc/meaning/05/meaning- online-5.html#nechvatal.

[30] Duchamp's entire artistic activity since the "definitive incompletion" of the *Large Glass* in 1923 was an exercise in strategic invisibility, giving rise to objects and events which—because they were apparently too impermanent or unimportant or insubstantial, or because they eluded established genre conventions, or because they confused or diluted authorial identity—evaded recognition as "works of art."

[31] Félix Guattari said in his noteworthy book, *Chaosmosis: An Ethico-Aesthetic Paradigm*, the work of art, for those who use it, is an activity of unframing, of rupturing sense, of baroque proliferation or extreme impoverishment that leads to a recreation and a reinvention of the subject itself.

The art of noise marks a qualitative transformation into a non-place where being and non-being reverse into each other, unfolding out and enfolding in their respective outsides. This short-circuit causes a creative conflagration typical of the art of noise.

Let's consider the difference between noise art (based on an individual's inner vision) verses the monstrous mass machine data market,[32] with its digital functionalism. For me the difference is in looking *into* and projecting *onto* something—thereby discovering an emerging manifestation based in invisibility—as opposed to looking *at* something. In that sense it requires an active slow participation on the part of the viewer—and noise style demands as much. For me this requires the use of hidden mental participation and, as such, is now essential in our climate of monstrous mass media in that it plays against the grain of given objective consensus visibility.

I believe that Minóy's deep droning palimpsest soundscapes exemplify what I have been theorizing above, the aesthetics of an obscure *monster sacré*. They suggest a spectral relationship between landscape and sound that accomplishes sensations of haunting dark ambience. They provoke dense planes of feelings, disrupted and veined by withdrawal and partial absence. They suggest a poetics of night. And of difficulty—one that explores both the outer space of presence and the inner space of remembrance, where a haunting perspective shatters both linear temporality and accounts of embodied emplacement.

---

[32] To support all that digital activity, there are now more than three million data centers of widely varying sizes worldwide, according to figures from the International Data Corporation.

After After After Words

HYPER NOISE AESTHETICS

Annoyance and Its Allowances in the Age
of the Digital Surveillance State

Joseph Nechvatal

> Noise nourishes a new era.
> Michele Serres, *The Parasite*

Now I would like to look more specifically at the possibility of further developments in noise art aesthetics concerning where becoming-imperceptible and becoming-perceptible nimbly interact. As sketched out in my book *Immersion Into Noise*, the evolution of visual noise art develops from certain pre-historic cave areas and baroque grottoes, to certain levels of mannerist and counter-mannerist complexity, to noisy spatial renderings in various exuberant architectural styles, then into cubism, futurism, dada, fluxus and other 20th-century avant-garde movements, into the screech of technological noise art, and into the softness of software noise art aesthetics.

As noted earlier in my "After After Words," what is important in the art of noise aesthetics is its intentional and elongated invisibility[1] and enigma. That is why this subject is so hard to write about. The very topic is a very difficult one to pin down and make intelligible for good reason. The art of noise is an art of disbelief in habitual codes of practice and understanding. You must take the art of noise on its own terms or risk doing violence to the art.

Noise art is not a set of homogeneous practices, but a complex field converging around perceived weaknesses in the art system. Such a noisy hyper-cognitive stance happens when the particularity of electronic connectivity is seen as part of an accrual total system by virtue of its being connected to everything else—while remaining dissonant. Noise aesthetics is a complex and ambiguous political gazing, and its theory of an art of resistance and investigation would be increasingly valuable to an analytical social movement based on skepticism. This is so as it counters the effects of our age of simplification: effects which have resulted from the glut of consumer-oriented entertainment messages and political propaganda which the monstrous mass media feed us daily in the interests of corporate profit.

The noise art aesthetic of the *monster sacré* (read Minóy) is that of dissonant immersion into a maelstrom of glossolaliaic unintelligibility, chaos and exaltation. The art of noise style is a way of seeing/hearing that reverses the order of figure/ground[2] to ground/figure. It collapses being into non-

---

[1] This parallels the fact that in many data facilities, servers are loaded with applications and left to run indefinitely, even after nearly all users have vanished or new versions of the same programs are running elsewhere. At a certain point, no one is responsible anymore, because no one, absolutely no one, wants to go in that room and unplug a server.

[2] The characteristic organization of perception into a figure that

being (ontological implosion). It creates ambivalent aleatory[3] processes that are true to our inner essential world: dynamic pools of expansion and disintegration.

The art of noise is that screech amid the collapse and extension of aesthetics connected to immanence and transcendence (where art is in the process of becoming-imperceptible-perceptible), facing the merging of figure into environment and environment into figure. We can find moments of this screech of collapse-extension in contemporary complexity theory and in some areas of information technology, nano-technology, cognitive science, and biotechnology. These moments of collapse-extension accompany the contemporary development where the static image has become dynamically engaged with the human imagination and personal choices of the viewer—in some cases, literally engaging the participation of the viewer (who becomes what I have elsewhere renamed as the *viewpant*)[4] to the point of physical interactivity. In other cases they are engaged conceptually (or post-conceptually) by looking long and hard at the art. I believe that the forms of this aesthetic post-conceptual participation can be a decisive element in

---

"stands out" against an undifferentiated background, e.g., a printed word against a background page. What is figural at any one moment depends on patterns of sensory stimulation and on the momentary interests of the perceiver.

[3] Aleatoricism is the incorporation of chance into the process of creation, especially the creation of art or media. The word derives from the Latin word *alea*, the rolling of dice.

[4] See Joseph Nechvatal, *Immersive Ideals/Critical Distances* (Lambert Academic Publishing, 2009), 56. One of the wider implications for art in viractual space is the proclivity to solicit the theoretical viewer/participant (what I call the "viewpant") to respond to the work in both a contemplative and physical way, or at least in an implied tension between these two poles when one side outweighs the other. It is important to remember that the viewpant is involved often with a series of different levels of immersion in a dynamic emergent continuum.

offering generative possibilities of development that will continue to be interesting and supportive of the gazing-commons.

The unwanted becoming-perceptible trend is likewise evident if we consider another aspect: the spread through social media technologies of content that uses visualization and data monitoring—for example, systems that survey and process in real-time preferences and movements of view-pants via mobile networks. So process-based data monitoring design and algorithmic architecture have now passed through the experimental phase and begun to have anti-commons practical uses. What we have witnessed for art through this development, coupled with relational art aesthetics, is on the one hand a spilling over towards entertainment, and on the other a growing integration with fast data monitoring surveillance.

In defense of the individual-based commons, my theory of the aesthetics of an art of noise encourages data monitoring *deferral*, where the search is rewarding in itself. Seen as too *difficult* by some, for me the paucity of clean art at a fast glance conceals the riches of associational gazing with respect to the combinatory dynamics of leisurely layered creations (read/hear Minóy).

In that regard, consider the large quantities of subtle kinds of noise that have proliferated since electricity, especially so since the onset of the information revolution at the end of the 1970s. With it came a low impact noise emitted by every kind of electrical appliance, contributing to the white-noise dense texture of our acoustic environment.[5] Such a post-industrial white noise environment is ambiguously omnipresent and mostly subliminal.

My suggestion for art noise aesthetics is, I believe, fully

---

[5] For more on this see R. Murray Schafer, *The Soundscape: Our Sonic Environment and the Tuning of the World* (Rochester, VT: Destiny Books, 1994).

able to render sensible the white noise sequencing when it uses subliminal latent excess in its presentational mode. Because such an excess overload of representation offers us a measure of freedom of choice in how we unpack it (or not). The greater amount of stimulation-information needed,[6] the greater the uncertainty that the "message" (proposition) offers. That is why my preference has been for semi-abstract, palimpsest-like work, like Minóy's, that contains subliminal latent excess. It has greater freedom of choice, and greater uncertainty, due to an excess of information via the ground/figure catastrophic collapse.

My concern here is with the ethical and liberating use of representation (and anti-representation) within the broader image environment. In attempting to represent the *monster sacré* aesthetic as non-representable (because the hugeness of post-industrial white noise is ubiquitous and subtlely present), art should obliterate the proper object of re-representation. This stress on the alterity and ineffability of noise that eludes our fuzzy grasp is what *hyper-noise* art is about.

The term *hyper-noise* is my theory of noise art as constructed via connected-competing vectors and figure/grounds.[7] This concept owes something to Quentin Meillassoux's idea of *hyper-Chaos* that was sketched out in his book *After Finitude*: a form of absolutization where nothing is impossible or unthinkable.[8] It must be grasped that hyper-Chaos is not just disorder, but that it also may produce order and stability, even little static worlds, as well as the complete destruction of what is.

Hyper-noise art refuses easy consumption and encourages love, because a love for noise art will make perturbing

---

[6] The New York Stock Exchange produces up to 2,000 gigabytes of data per day that must be stored for years.

[7] Joseph Nechvatal, *Immersion Into Noise* (Ann Arbor: Open Humanities Press/MPublishing, 2011), 31.

[8] Quentin Meillassoux, *After Finitude: An Essay on the Necessity of Contingency*, trans. Ray Brassier (London: Continuum, 2008), 64.

events in your life more tolerable. It will make you able to see and hear more and make you more adaptable to disturbance, rather than being torn up about them. It will help you to avoid psychic ossification by loving latent expanse. Hyper-noise art can thus be referred to the aesthetics of the *sublime*, which, in the 18th century, was connected with the grandness of natural phenomena.

Generative hyper-noise art is perhaps the most evident example of this hyper-noise sublime opportunity, as post-conceptual generative art serves to produce unpredictable results, both when it is based on arithmetic instructions contained in code, or in other ritual rules. So hyper-noise software art means primarily some form of generative or semi-generative art, in which the artist establishes the operational tenets/choices that are calculated to act autonomously or semi-autonomously.

The above-mentioned white-hyper-noise dense texture of our acoustic environment, with its uniformity and lack of variance, suggests to me a possibility of connecting ourselves psychically to the great chain of being (that which proceeds us and of which we are a part) through contemporary art. However, this requires an active imagination that is aided by the visualization properties offered up in the art of noise.

This potential of noise art aesthetics is embedded in the recognition of our sheer potentiality: all the selves we have within to develop or burn out. All the worlds we might create or destroy. Hyper-noise art shows us that we are more diverse than we had imagined, and more tolerant. It points out that what we have in common is a dangerous propensity for overrating our powers of comprehension.

But noise art aesthetics is hostile to generalizations. It is recalcitrant by design. It affirms with jubilation our state of varied mutability. That is my general standard of excellence for it.

Noise art aesthetics tears our phallogocentricism apart to confront the diversity in us, and in each other. This lesson is a necessity and the recognition of this necessity is part of the peculiar pleasure that noise art affords us—a pleasure clearly of rapturous abandonment where the intended effect is an inner liberation by means of de-simulation. Noise art aesthetics opens up in us a sense of possibility that we understand and feel at one and the same time to be both dangerous and indispensable. It points us towards the perilous turbulences and chancy exhilarations that pass through us: overcast, heartbroken, eloquent passages that pull us apart even as they discharge pent-up repressed forms of accepted common wisdom. So, my initiative for a hyper-noise art aesthetic is not a swoon to an intricate inner violence. Rather, it has the look and sound more of analogue: like that of the delicately puckered anus that we each own but do not face to a cosmogony of expanding orifice that keeps reminding us that we were left behind.

So noise aesthetics is a return to the shifting ground on which music and art rests. The art of noise gives us a sense of discovery that marked music and art's beginning. It is an alternative, phantasmagorical way to express the agitation between form and the ground. It dislodges art and music from their customary formal frameworks and makes them thrillingly intense again. The art of noise is beautiful negativity.

But understanding noise aesthetics may be too limited a goal here, as the art of noise attempts to expresses the unsayable. Or perhaps all it says is: WAKE THE FUCK UP (sounding a wake-up call). But that is far from nothing. So perhaps this idea of an art of noise is a psychotic outburst that disrupts smooth image operations with an explosion of buried visual hysteria that promises a highly diverse world.

Its incomprehensibility by design connects the commons to our unconscious mind and inner feelings through what I think to be a type of chaos magic.[9] Through a variety of

---

[9] Some common sources of inspiration for chaos magic include

techniques often reminiscent of Western ceremonial magic or indigenous shamanism, many practitioners of chaos magic believe they can change both their subjective experience and objective reality. Although there are a few techniques unique to chaos magic (such as some forms of sigil magic[10]), chaos magic is often highly individualistic and borrows liberally from other belief systems. In this way, some chaos magicians consider their practice to be a meta-belief.

Chaoist noise art creates the visualization bridge between form and intuition, as its uncertain images have more information in them than a clear certain image (or sound) has, where the information quickly becomes redundant. Thus noise art gives rise to new thought. It promotes the emergence of new forms of an old story: art.

As mentioned above, what is important in the art of noise is its intentional enigma. It needs to be obscure to the degree that its codes cannot be discerned. This phantasmagorical obscurity and mystery is desirable in a world that has become increasingly data-mined, mapped, quantified, specialized, and identified in a straightforward matter-of-fact way. This will for enigma is the basis for discovering and entering into an immersion into the art of noise.[11]

---

such diverse areas as science fiction, scientific theories, ceremonial magic, shamanism, Eastern philosophy, and individual experimentation.

[10] The sigil concept was mostly popularized by the artist Austin Osman Spare, who published a method by which the words of a statement of intent are reduced into an abstract design; the sigil is then charged with the will of the creator. Spare's technique, now known as sigilization, has become a core element of chaos magic. For more on Austin Osman Spare, see my essay "On Austin Osman Spare," in Joseph Nechvatal, *Towards an Immersive Intelligence: Essays on the Work of Art in the Age of Computer Technology and Virtual Reality (1993–2006)* (New York City: Edgewise Press. 2009), 40–52.

[11] As an example, see/hear Marina Rosenfeld's *Cephissus landscape*

Such aesthetic enigma is alluring when intelligible mining-type data processing is perceived as hollow, trite, and insensitive. Its goal is to disrupt instrumental logic and contradict, counteract, and cancel out false reason and hollow feeling.

What also interests me profoundly with art of noise aesthetics is the extent to which it urges the mind towards transformations. Here art is the infinite space of hyper-chaos imagination. A hyper-chaos art noise includes principles of networked connections and electronic links that give multiple choices of passages to follow and continually new branching possibilities. Instead of stressing the reflective limits imposed by the category of art, the art of noise aesthetic may attempt to specify the resistance embodied within it. So noise art's counter to the spectacle's misery consists in not forgetting or denying spectacle, but in an interruption of it with a phantasmagorical semi-remembering of pre-spectacular suffering through which human grief is at one and the same time relived and relieved. Suffering and joy, like figure and ground, are here tied together, neither one without the other. Thus noise art aesthetics suggest and produce stress in us—one might even say an urgent anxiety of disintegration. So dedication to its merits, if there are any, might well be described as vaguely heroic, because noise art aesthetics suggests the revelation of a plentiful nihilistic life force. Thus noise art aesthetics can be as creative as it is destructive. Or they imply an endless struggle between the two. In that sense it is a cul-de-sac of ill communication (vacuole)[12]—the communication of enigma it-

---

(2002), an immersive noise work that undermines the central notion of "surround-sound" technology by locating viewers in an environment with no fixed center and numerous temporary sonic sweet spots where short bursts of mingled electronic and acoustic sounds intersect and decay in expanding concentric circles that suggest oscillate landscapes.

[12] This is a reference to Gilles Deleuze's (1925-1995) notion of the

self.

Indeed, phantasmagorical falsifications of the self (again, read/hear Minóy) are highlighted by noise art's non-representation ability—its refusal to participate in the world of the clear and precise, with its massive data banks, clone-like lifestyle models and ideological conceptual camps. When we have become too complicated to clarify and order, but too accepting of the administrations of our existence, noise art aesthetics offers a certain path of socially acceptable withdrawal. I mean here a boomeranging figure/ground withdrawal that provides the means for secretly re-identifying ourselves.

So noise art experience has something that words risk diminishing. Nevertheless, I obviously have felt that I must take that risk because if we are to continue to live among electronic vibrations that mine us, it may be helpful to talk back against them. But yes, noise art aesthetics is the transmitter of unspeakable secrets. That is why art noise matters. It wants *more* from us. Moreover, it teaches us *to want more from art*. It teaches us to look *deeper*, to hear *more*, and to trust the inner noise.

---

vacuole. This concept of noncommunication comes from Gilles Deleuze, "Postscript on the Societies of Control," *October* 59 (Winter 1992): 3–7. Deleuze's notion of control is connected to information-communication technology—a concept he pulled out of the work of William S. Burroughs (1914-1997). A vacuole is like a sac in a cell's membrane, completely bound up inside the cell but also separate from it. Vacuoles play a significant role in autophagy, maintaining an *imbalance* between biogenesis (production) and *degradation* (or turnover) of many substances and cell structures. They also aid in the destruction of invading bacteria or of misfolded proteins that have begun to build up within the cell. The vacuole is a major part of the plant and animal cell. See also Nechvatal, *Immersion Into Noise*, 14.

W. dreams, like Phaedrus, of an army of thinker-friends, thinker-lovers. He dreams of a thought-army, a thought-pack, which would storm the philosophical Houses of Parliament. He dreams of Tartars from the philosophical steppes, of thought-barbarians, thought-outsiders. What distance would shine in their eyes!

~Lars Iyer

www.babelworkinggroup.org

www.ingramcontent.com/pod-product-compliance
Lightning Source LLC
Chambersburg PA
CBHW070848160426
43192CB00012B/2362